R

Post-Brexit Britain

by

Christopher J. Armstrong

Anthony Piccolo

Gen'ichiro Itakura

SHOHAKUSHA

はじめに

この20年の間に、イギリスのイメージは大きく変わった。

確かに、ハリー・ポッターと〈ファンタスティック・ビースト〉のシリーズは人気があるし、シャーロック・ホームズやアリス、サッカーやアフタヌーン・ティーもよく知られている。

だが、2020年のEU（ヨーロッパ連合）離脱に見られるように、この国は大きな変動のさなかにある。国民の分断が報じられるようになったが、それは21世紀に始まったものではない。マーガレット・サッチャーとトニー・ブレアによって押し進められた新自由主義は格差を拡大し、大多数の国民が誇りに思っている福祉国家政策は危機に瀕している。2022年にリシ・スナクがインド系イギリス人初の首相となったことでわかりにくくなったが、人種や信仰に基づく差別は根強く残り、一部は安全保障の名の下に正当化されている。これに加え、ジェンダーについての考えの違いから、「フェミニスト」を名乗る人たちの間で激しい衝突が起こっている。それが、現在のイギリスの姿なのだ。

本書は、現代のイギリスの諸相を批評的に見直すものである。収録された15のエッセイのトピックは、EU離脱、王室風刺、アイルランド紛争の記憶、環境問題、音楽やSNS、格差社会、ウィンドラッシュ事件、ジェンダー・セクシュアリティと多岐にわたる。イギリス映画、テレビ番組、ネット配信番組を参照しながらも、「緊縮ノスタルジア」や「TERF」といった新しい言葉を積極的に取り入れ、近年のドキュメンタリー、学術論文・研究書、社会評論なども適宜紹介している。イギリス文化・社会研究の導入としてもお読みいただければと考えている。

語学教材として、本書は学習者のレベルとニーズに応じて異なる使い方ができる。各章は以下のように構成されている。

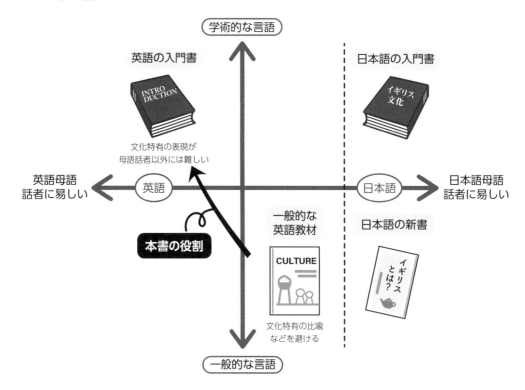

1. **Brainstorming on the Topic** では、トピックについて知っていることをどんどん挙げていくことで他の学生と知識を共有する
2. **Vocabulary** では、エッセイやリスニングで用いられている語彙を習得する
3. **Reading Comprehension** では、600 語程度のエッセイを読み、TOEFL iBT® および IELTS™ 形式の問題を解くことで読解力を高める
4. **Listening Comprehension** では、本文に関連する会話や講義や発表を聞くことでリスニング能力を高める
5. **Discussion** にはエッセイを自分なりに評価したり、関連するトピックについて自分の意見を述べたりすることで英語力のみならず考える力も養える
6. **Homework/Research** では、関連する映画などを視聴することで取り上げられた題材についての理解をより深いものにできる

♣凡例♣ 本書で用いられている略称は以下の通り。

名 →名詞　自動 →自動詞　他動 →他動詞　形 →形容詞　副 →副詞　対 →対義語

　各章に Vocabulary と TOEFL iBT® および IELTS™ の形式に準拠した Reading Comprehension があり、語彙の増強やテストのスコアの向上という明快な目標をもって学習を続けることができる。また、Listening Comprehension を併用すれば、総合的な英語力の向上にも役立てられる。

　一方で、本書はリーディングとリスニング以外にも多くのアクティビティも用意している。読んだ内容やそこで使われた言葉を自分のものにするためには、実際に使用してみることも大切である。また、自分でも調査や、クリエイティブな活動(本書の Homework/Research にはイラストやビデオ作成も含まれる) をすることで、内容を多面的に理解することができるだろう。

　本書でも取り上げている AI の普及や教育利用については様々な意見があるだろうが、今後は標準化されたテスト問題を解く能力よりも問題発見能力やクリエイティブな能力——もしくはクリエイティブな「プロンプト」を作る能力——の育成が教育現場に求められていくだろう。本書がそういったニーズにも応えてくれることを願っている。なお、教授用資料には評価方法などのアイデアを提示している。

　Discussion や Homework/Research は、学習者の専門分野に応じて難易度を上げることもできる。このアクティビティだけに特化して、本書をイギリス文化・社会研究に関わる講義やゼミの副教材として使用してもよい。英語での授業の増加に伴い、語学と講義の橋渡しをする教材は増えている。だが、語学教材が学術用語を用いたり、最新の研究を反映したりすることはまだ多くない。オックスフォード大学出版局の *Very Short Introductions* など、英語で書かれた入門書は英語母語話者をターゲットにしたものがほとんどで、日本の学習者にとってはハードルが高い。本書はこの「橋渡し」を目指すものである。

　なお、本書の作成には松柏社の森有紀子氏ならびに永野啓子氏にお世話になった。森氏の呼びかけがあってこそ本書は生まれたのだし、編集作業での永野氏の的確な助言や指摘がなければ本書は形にならなかった。ここに謝意を表したい。

2023 年 10 月　筆者一同

Reading Post-Brexit Britain

Contents

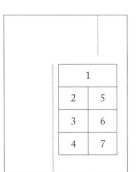

📷 Cover photos 🖼

1. Panoramic view of the skyline of London, UK. © Sven Hansche / Shutterstock.com
2. Larry the Downing Street cat and Chief Mouser to the Treasury outside Number 10 Downing Street.
©Tommy London / Alamy Stock Photo
3. London—Tooting High Street, South West London. © William Barton / Shutterstock.com
4. The Barter Books library at Alnwick, Northumberland, England, UK. ©David Dixon / Alamy Stock Photo
5. The Jacobite Express (The train made famous as the Hogwarts Express in the Harry Potter films)
crosses the Glenfinnan Viaduct in the Scottish High lands. ©bradley page / Alamy Stock Photo
6. People walking along the River Thames on the South Bank, South Bank, London, UK. ©Steve Tulley /
Alamy Stock Photo
7. London, UK. November 21, 2018. Red placard with the slogan 'Brexit: is it worth it?' seen in central
London at a protest.©Joe Kuis / Shutterstock.com

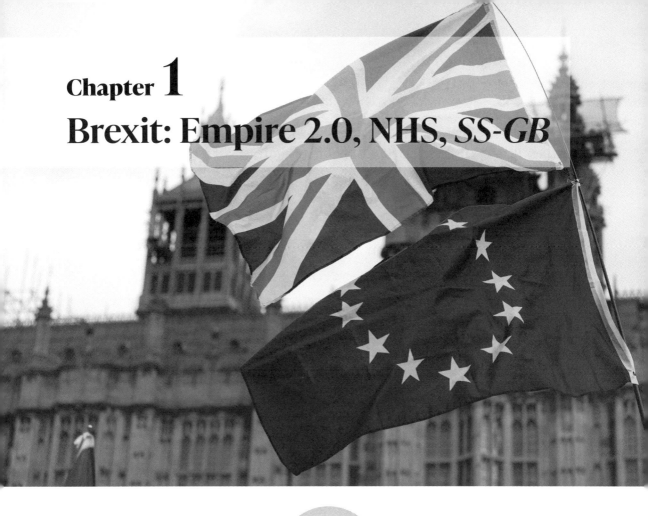

Chapter 1
Brexit: Empire 2.0, NHS, *SS-GB*

Warming-Up Activities

1. Brainstorming on the Topic

「ブレグジット」（イギリスの EU 離脱）について知っていることを書き出してみよう。そもそも EU（ヨーロッパ連合）とはどのような組織で、その加盟国にはどのような恩恵と義務があるのだろう？　また、その前身は何だったのだろう？　イギリスはいつそこに加わり、いつそこから出ることになったのだろう？

2. Vocabulary

☐ referendum 名 国民投票、住民投票

☐ integration 名 統合

☐ immigration 名 移民（> immigrant）

☐ imperialist 形 帝国主義的な（> imperialism）

☐ nostalgia 名 ノスタルジア（形 nostalgic）

☐ Welfare State 福祉国家

☐ colony 名 植民地

☐ consensus 名 コンセンサス、合意

☐ recession 名 不景気

☐ coincidence 名（自動 coincide (with...)）

On 31 January 2020, the UK left the European Union (EU). Four years earlier, Prime Minister David Cameron announced a referendum on whether Britain should remain in or leave the EU. Although he supported 'Remain', he added the referendum to his election manifesto, partly because of pressure from
5 a 'Eurosceptic' group of his own party, the Conservative Party. 'Euroscepticism' refers to various political positions. Some people simply criticise problems in the EU's specific policies, but others reject European integration. The second stance, or 'hard Euroscepticism', was a driving force of the 'Leave'
10 campaign. Neither the Conservative leader nor the Labour leader— Labour being the major opposition party—officially supported Leave, so it seemed to people outside the
15 UK that hard Eurosceptics had

no chance. They did not look great, either. They insisted they should reduce immigration and some harassed migrant workers from the EU, especially Polish. Naturally, the result of the referendum shocked the world: 51.9% voted in favour of leaving the EU. Why did it happen?

20 The rise of hard Euroscepticism has been commonly explained in two ways: imperialist nostalgia and patriotic defence of the Welfare State. Historian Arnold Toynbee once remarked that the British people 'won not only the Commonwealth but the Welfare State'. Despite its World War II victory, Britain went bankrupt and lost its colonies. And yet it managed to create the Commonwealth of Nations,
25 an association mainly made up of many of the former British colonies. By leaving the EU, some believed, Britain would strengthen its ties with Commonwealth members and thereby create 'Empire 2.0', or a new version of British Empire. Their claim hardly sounds original. In the 1960s, many used the same logic and opposed the government's proposal to enter the European Economic Community (EEC)—
30 which would later become the EU. Even if this nostalgia only fascinated people on the right, the story of the imperilled Welfare State caused more widespread alarm. In the 1940s, the Labour government established a consensus with the

Conservatives to create a Welfare State, and founded the National Health Service (NHS), which provided free healthcare services for all ordinary residents of the UK. Regardless of their political positions, many British people believe that the NHS is what they must be proud of and they must defend no matter what. Many Leave campaigners openly accused not only immigrants but also 'health tourists' of draining the NHS of its precious resources.

According to Fintan O'Toole's *Heroic Failure* (2019), however, these two alone may not have had enough appeal. He added another fantasy—that of Nazi-occupied Britain—to his long list of factors. Needless to say, Britain defeated the Nazis in 1945. But look, some thought, the tables turned. While Britain was still unable to drag itself out of recession, Germany achieved *Wirtschaftswunder*, or an economic miracle, and became a major membership state of the EEC. As a new member, the UK had to accept Germany's terms and conditions. In 1975, Labour MP Peter Shore remarked that it was 'almost as though we had

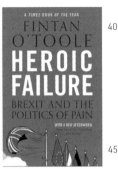

Heroic Failure: Brexit and the Politics of Pain (Apollo Publishers, 2018)

suffered a defeat in a war'. Many politicians compared Britain's 1973 entry into the EEC with its 1938 approval of Hitler's ambition. The bestseller at that time was Len Deighton's *SS-GB* (1978), which depicts an alternative history of Britain after its surrender to the Nazis. In the 2010s, the Leave campaigner Roger Helmer emphasised that his parents' generation fought the war to make sure that their children should not be German citizens, asking why they have to remain 'European' citizens. In short, they imagine themselves fighting the Nazis, now renamed EU. Or they still cannot wake up from this nightmare of occupied Britain. Just before the 2016 referendum, the BBC announced its plan to adapt *SS-GB* for television. Was it really a coincidence?

NOTES

l. 4: **manifesto** 名 マニフェスト、政権公約
l. 5: **Conservative Party** 保守党 (イギリスの二大政党の一つ)
l. 5: **Euroscepticism** 名 ヨーロッパ統合懐疑派
l. 11: **Labour (Party)** 労働党 (イギリスの二大政党の一つ)
l. 24: **Commonwealth of Nations** イギリス連邦
l. 29: **European Economic Community** ヨーロッパ経済共同体
l. 31: **imperilled > imperil** 他動 ～を危うくする、～を危険にさらす
ll. 33-34: **National Health Service** 国民健康保険サービス
l. 48: **MP** 国会議員 (**Member of Parliament**)
l. 51: **alternative** 形 代替の、既存のものとは別の

1. According to paragraph 1, which of the following statements is true?

   (A) The UK decided not to withdraw from the EU as the prime minister wanted.

   (B) Hard Eurosceptics demanded political reform within the EU.

   (C) The prime minister promised to hold a general vote if he won the election.

   (D) It came as no surprise to foreigners that Britain decided to leave the EU.

2. In paragraph 2, the author cites Arnold Toynbee in order to show

   (A) what exactly the Commonwealth and the Welfare State are in the first place.

   (B) when the government created the Commonwealth and the Welfare State.

   (C) why the creation of the Commonwealth deterred that of the Welfare State.

   (D) how British people are proud of the Commonwealth and the Welfare State.

3. In paragraph 2, the author implies that

   (A) Commonwealth member states should contribute to Britain as did British colonies.

   (B) even in the 1960s, many people thought they should turn to the Commonwealth, not Europe.

   (C) Empire 2.0 appealed to a wider range of people than the Welfare State.

   (D) The Leave campaign was propelled by people on the left who loved the Welfare State.

4. According to paragraph 3, all of the following statements are true EXCEPT:

   (A) Many British believed they were still occupied by the Nazis.

   (B) Many British people felt uncomfortable with Germany's success in the post-war era.

   (C) Many British people hated to follow the dictates of the country they beat.

   (D) Many British people thought it would be horrible to live under the Nazi rule.

5.–7. Complete the timeline below. Use one word only from the passage for each answer.

1945   Britain ^{5.}_____ the Second World War

1940s   The British government created the NHS

1950s   Britain lost its economic power and many of its ^{6.}_____ began to win their independence, though many remained in the Commonwealth of Nations

1960s   Germany made a successful ^{7.}_____ recovery

The British government tried to join the EEC

1973   Britain became a member state of the EEC

2016   Britain held a referendum to decide whether it should leave the EU

2020   Britain left the EU

Listening Comprehension ////

🔊 Audio 1-03

Listen to the conversation between two students, Emma and Max, about the reading passage. Answer whether the following statements are **true** or **false**.

1. Max initially felt upset.   [   ]

2. Emma is confident that hard Eurosceptics are heading in the right direction.   [   ]

3. During the conversation, Emma and Max ended up hating each other.   [   ]

1. Listen to the dialogue again. Exactly what issue do you think Emma has chosen for her presentation? Or what issue would you choose if you were Emma?

2. There are many alternative World War II history novels like *SS-GB* (e.g. Robert Harris' *Fatherland* (1992)). Many of them have been adapted for film or television. Britain won the war. Why do you think British people want to read such novels?

Homework/Research ///

Fintan O'Toole cites five more factors in *Heroic Failure*. One of them is the cult of 'heroic failure' in British—especially English—culture. Historical events such as the Charge of the Light Brigade (Crimean War) have inspired patriotism and yet have been a subject of caricature.

Create a poster, a cartoon or an artwork about one of those events (the Charge of the Light Brigade, Scott of Antarctica, the flight from Dunkirk and Brexit). You can work in pairs or groups. For example:

"It's madness, sir." "Don't worry. We have a poet. Your glory cannot fade."

Chapter 2
Political Satire in the UK

Warming-Up Activities

1. Brainstorming on the Topic

政治風刺についてどんなことを知っているだろう？　政治風刺は権力者に影響を与える方法として有効だろうか？　以下の Vocabulary から二つ以上の語を選んでブレインストーミングをし、ディスカッションしてみよう。

2. Vocabulary

☐ satire 名 風刺

☐ social media ソーシャルメディア、SNS

☐ ridicule 名 嘲り 他動 〜をあざ笑う

☐ exaggeration 名 誇張（他動 exaggerate）

☐ sarcasm 名 皮肉、嫌み（形 sarcastic）

☐ austerity 名 緊縮財政

☐ affluence 名 富裕

☐ ironically 副 皮肉なことに（名 irony）

☐ apathy 名 無感動、冷淡

☐ cynicism 名 冷笑、シニシズム

The animated satire *The Prince* aired for one season on HBO Max before being cancelled in February 2022 amidst largely negative reviews. The series, created by American Gary Janetti and featuring the voices of a star-studded British and American cast, focuses on the life of eight-year-old Prince George, son of
5 Prince William and Kate Middleton and third in line to the throne. Those who know the British tabloid press did not find much to be shocked about. Yet a swift backlash emerged in the press and in social media, with Britons calling the series 'cruel' and in poor taste for making a child the focus of the series. According to Carolyn Harris, a royal historian, the reaction may be due to the difficulty that
10 Prince William and Prince Harry experienced growing up with constant media attention. Britons, she suggested, believe that the privacy of the royal children needs to be protected. Others insisted that the show was just not funny—not for British audiences anyway. Full of American cultural references, the series seemed to miss every opportunity to till the rich soil of the monarchy for comedy and satire.

15 Satire of royalty—and of politicians—has been a staple of British public life for centuries. Works of satire, including poems, songs, paintings and drawing, novels, television and film, use derisive humour, ridicule, exaggeration and sarcasm, to attack immoral conduct and stupidity among the powerful. In the 18th century, satire was indeed cruel, graphic and personal; no one was spared the satirist's pen,
20 as the 2010 BBC series *Rude Britannia* tells us. Satire re-emerged in the UK in the 1960s as wartime austerity gave way to affluence and permissiveness—and as the collapse of the British empire accelerated. The comedy revue *Beyond the Fringe*, the TV programme *That Was the Week That Was* and the magazine *Private Eye* were the cutting edge of a 'satire boom' that took aim at 'the establishment'. Ironically,
25 the leaders of the boom were Oxbridge products, members of that same class they satirised. During the 1980s, it was a crowd of ugly latex puppets on a satirical TV show called *Spitting Image* (1984–96) that got Britons laughing—attracting 15 million viewers at the height of its popularity. *Spitting Image* was rebooted in 2020, with PM Boris Johnson leading the cast of puppets.

30 But how much work do satirists have to do given such clownish leaders as Boris Johnson? Novelist Jonathan Coe famously remarked that Johnson was 'his own satirist'—and quite calculating in his buffoonery, according to Coe, because

he understood that 'the best way to make sure the satire aimed at you is gentle and unchallenging is to create it yourself'. Johnson's ministers and successors, reportedly dim and incompetent, also make satirists redundant. With such incompetent leaders and such clownish behaviour, it's no wonder that a recent report entitled *Political Disengagement in the UK* found that trust in politicians is at an all-time low, fallen from a mere 38% in 1986 to 17% in 2013 to a dismal 9% currently. 35

The Windsors is a hit television satire that, in the words of one reviewer, portrays the royal family as 'uncomplicated, two-dimensional, doltish, pointless figures'. First aired in 2016, the show is wildly popular, and is reportedly enjoyed by some of the royals themselves, including Prince William and Kate Middleton. In the lead up to the Coronation of Charles III at Westminster Abbey on 9 May, 2023, *The Windsors* broadcast a Coronation Special—earning high praise from fans and reviewers. In the episode, PM Rishi Sunak informs Charles the country cannot afford a lavish ceremony, but Charles wants a 'mega-coronation'. When a 'budget coronation' is booked instead, Charles gives up the throne to William. Yet the public want the real thing, and the coronation of Charles goes ahead. *The Windsors* proves that, in good times and bad, making fun of the royals is an essential British pastime. 40 45 50

NOTES

l. 1: **HBO Max** HBOマックス (アメリカ合衆国のオンデマンド動画配信サービス)
l. 2: **amidst** 前 ～の真ん中で、～のさなかに
l. 3: **star-studded** 形 スターでいっぱいの、豪華キャストの
l. 6: **tabloid** 名 タブロイド (しばしば煽情的な記事を載せる大衆紙)
l. 14: **till the rich soil** 豊かな土壌を耕す (比喩的に用いられていることに注意)
l. 14: **monarchy** 名 王政
l. 17: **derisive** 形 愚弄的な
l. 22: **revue** 名 レビュー (寸劇や歌などからなるミュージカルコメディのような演目)
l. 25: **Oxbridge** オックスフォード大学やケンブリッジ大学出身者 (の) (ともにイギリスのエリート大学)
l. 26: **latex** 名 ラテックス、ゴム製品
l. 28: **rebooted > reboot** 他動 ～を再起動する、再始動する
l. 29: **PM = prime minister** 内閣総理大臣
l. 30: **clownish** 形 道化のような
l. 32: **buffoonery** 名 道化、おどけ、悪ふざけ
l. 37: **disengagement** 名 解放、解約、離脱
l. 38: **dismal** 形 陰鬱な、惨憺たる
l. 40: **doltish** 形 間抜けな
l. 43: **coronation** 名 戴冠、戴冠式
l. 46: **lavish** 形 物惜しみのない、贅沢な

1. *The Prince* experienced a backlash in the UK press and in social media because

   (A) the voice actors were all American.

   (B) the series often relied on references to American, rather than British culture.

   (C) the story focuses on a child, Prince George, third in line to the throne.

   (D) it was not funny.

2.–5. Do the following statements agree with the information given in the passage? Write **true** (the statement agrees with the information), **false** (the statement contradicts the information) or **not given** (there is no information on this).

   2. The idea for *The Prince* evolved out of creator Gary Janetti's Instagram account.

   3. The leaders of the 'satire boom' of the 1960s were members of the class that they criticised.

   4. *Spitting Image* attracted fifteen million British viewers for its 2020 reboot.

   5. *The Windsors* special episode on the coronation of King Charles III was panned by critics.

6. According to paragraph 2,

   (A) the successors of PM Boris Johnson have the confidence of the British public.

   (B) trust in Britain's leaders is lower than it has ever been.

   (C) Johnson is both unintelligent and incompetent.

   (D) Johnson likes to write satire.

7. According to the passage, *The Windsors*

   (A) depicts the members of the royal family as shallow and foolish.

   (B) is a satire of PM Rishi Sunak's Conservative government.

   (C) is watched and enjoyed by King Charles III.

   (D) was criticized for making fun of Prince George.

Listening Comprehension

📶 Audio 1-05

Listen to a student discuss an article about contemporary British political satire. Answer whether the following statements are **true** or **false**.

1. The student has read an article that criticises the commonly held view about the role of satire in politics.   [   ]

2. According to the student, the authors of the article believe satire creates cynicism and apathy among citizens.   [   ]

3. According to the student's understanding, comedy and satire are not outside politics; they are part of it.   [   ]

Discussion ////

1. Considering what you have read and heard in this unit, do you think satire is an effective way to bring about political change? Is it merely part of the spectacle of modern politics? What can we learn from the study of political satire?

2. Think about a political leader that you admire, past and present. What qualities in leaders can build trust among the public? Make a list of these qualities and discuss them with classmates.

Homework/Research ////

1. Investigate the satire boom in Britain in the 1950s and 60s. Why did young educated Britons criticise members of their own class?

2. Choose one of the following British politicians and research their background and political careers: David Cameron, Theresa May, Boris Johnson, Liz Truss or Rishi Sunak. How have they been treated by the media?

Chapter 3
Britain, Ireland and the Great Hunger

Warm-Up Activities

1. Brainstorming on the Topic

現在飢饉に苦しんでいる国や地域について知っていることを挙げてみよう。また、過去に飢饉に苦しんでいた国や地域についてはどうだろう？　飢饉をなくそうとする国際的な人道支援については？　また、神経的過食症や神経的拒食症などの摂食障害についてはどんなことを知っているだろう？

2. Vocabulary

□ **famine** 名 飢饉、飢餓

□ **devastate** 他動 ～を荒廃させる（>devastation）

□ **emigrate** 自動 移住する、出国する

□ **inadequate** 形 不適当な（対 adequate）

□ **malicious** 名 悪意のある

□ **fast** 自動 断食する。絶食する

□ **pervade** 他動 ～に普及する、広がる

□ **nourishment** 名 栄養、食物

□ **grieve** 自動 他動 深く悲しむ、悲しませる

□ **repent** 自動 他動 後悔する、悔い改める

The Irish Potato Famine (also referred to as the Great Famine or the Great Hunger) devastated Ireland in the mid-19th century. From 1845 to 1852 a potato blight destroyed approximately three-fourths of Ireland's potato crop (the staple food for the majority of the population). During the seven years of the famine, 5 more than one million Irish died. Over the following years, another one to two million Irish people emigrated, resulting in a loss of almost 25% of the population. The negative effects of such drastic demographic change would continue to be felt far into the 20th century and beyond. For many Irish, what would be remembered was not only the famine itself but also the response of the British Parliament 10 during the famine—seen by most as inadequate at best and malicious at worst.

The memory and ongoing cultural presence of the famine can be seen as recently as 2022 in the Irish film *The Wonder* (based on the novel by Emma Donoghue). As the movie begins, we hear a character offscreen telling us: 'It is 1862. We left England bound for Ireland. The Great Famine still casts a long 15 shadow and the Irish hold England responsible for that devastation.' We see a young woman sitting, eating, at a table in the hold of a ship. She is Elizabeth Wright, an English nurse who has been hired to come to a small village in Ireland to keep watch for two weeks over Anna O'Donnell, a young girl who claims to have not eaten for four months since her 11th birthday, yet appears to be healthy 20 and thriving. The village is being overrun by gawkers and pilgrims who wish to witness first-hand 'the fasting girl'. The town fathers want to know if they have a *bona fide* miracle on their hands or a hoax. Elizabeth has no doubts that this is a hoax, but she is told that if Anna is not truly a 'wonder', then 'prove it'. And so the two-week watch begins with Elizabeth alternating eight-hour shifts with a 25 Catholic nun who is also a nurse.

Although *The Wonder* is not directly or primarily about the Great Famine, the story takes place in Ireland at a time when the famine is not yet just a memory. The survivors still live it. In an NPR interview in 2016, Emma Donoghue explained that she set the story in Ireland in the years immediately after the Great Famine 30 because 'I wanted to set the idea of voluntarily starving against the appalling context of involuntarily starving'. Reminders of the famine pervade the film. The village doctor, for example, lights vigil candles at a small altar in his home

The Wonder (Netflix, 2022)

for his deceased wife and children. Not stated directly, but strongly implied, is that they have died from the famine. 35 Elizabeth discovers that a journalist from London who has come to write about Anna was actually a local boy whose family died in the famine while he was away at boarding school. During 40 the famine his family had 'locked themselves up in their cabin . . . and nailed the door shut from the inside' to avoid the shame of dying in the street. And, as if to emphasise the extremes of 'feast or famine', scenes of Anna steadfastly not eating are interspersed with scenes of Elizabeth devouring bowls of stew at the boarding house or in the O'Donnell's kitchen. And when Elizabeth inadvertently removes 45 the source of nourishment that Anna has been secretly receiving, Anna begins to weaken, her previously 'miraculous' good health begins to fail, and she is now in danger of starving to death and becoming a very different kind of famine victim.

The movie ends with a return to the narrative frame of listening to the same offscreen character observing: 'Perhaps it is not a village that gathers to grieve 50 what it has lost and repent its sins of omission, nor a single nation. All over the empire, are not children left to lie down and die in ditches and gutters every night of the year?' In *The Wonder*, famine, Britain and empire are never very far away.

NOTES

l. 3: **blight** 名 胴枯れ病
l. 7: **drastic** 形 強烈な、徹底した
l. 7: **demographic** 形 人口統計上の
l. 20: **overrun** 他動 ～を荒らし回る
l. 20: **gawkers > gawker** 名 野次馬、興味本位の見物人
l. 20: **pilgrims > pilgrim** 名 巡礼者、参拝者
l. 22: ***bona fide*** 名 善意の、真正な
l. 28: **NPR** ナショナル・パブリック・ラジオ（アメリカ合衆国の非営利ラジオ放送局）
l. 32: **vigil candles** 名 （教会などで点す）小さいろうそく、常灯明
l. 32: **altar** 名 祭壇、聖餐台
l. 33: **deceased** 形 最近亡くなった、故～
l. 43: **steadfastly** 副 しっかりと
l. 44: **interspersed > intersperse** 他動 ～をまき散らす、散在させる
l. 44: **devouring > devour** 他動 ～をむさぼる
l. 45: **inadvertently** 副 知らずに

1. All of the following statements are true of the Irish Potato Famine EXCEPT:

   (A) The potato was the main food source for the majority of the Irish.

   (B) The response of the British government to the famine could have been better.

   (C) Over one million people left Ireland to escape the famine.

   (D) The effects of the famine were felt far beyond the seven years of the famine itself.

2. According to paragraph 2, Elizabeth Wright has been hired to

   (A) get Anna to start eating.

   (B) discover if Anna is eating.

   (C) stop Anna from eating.

   (D) keep Anna healthy.

3. The village doctor and the journalist from London are examples of

   (A) people who believe Anna's fasting is a hoax.

   (B) outsiders who do not understand Irish culture.

   (C) members of Anna's family who believe she is a 'wonder'.

   (D) people who have been directly affected by the famine.

4. The offscreen narration at the beginning and end of the film

   (A) provides some historical and cultural background to the story.

   (B) introduces the main characters and explains their relation to Anna.

   (C) explains the unique challenges involved in making the movie.

   (D) calls attention to the increasing prevalence of eating disorders.

5.–7. Complete the summary below. Choose one word only from the passage.

The story of *The Wonder* takes place in Ireland at a time before the Great Famine became just a **5.**_____. Those who have survived the famine still **6.**_____ with the effects of the famine. **7.**_____ of the Great Famine can be found throughout the film.

Listening Comprehension /////

🔊 **Audio 1-07**

Listen to the conversation between Angela and Mika about the reading passage. Answer whether the following statements are **true** or **false**.

1. Mika doesn't want to see the movie because it's too intense.   [   ]

2. *The Wonder* is about a Welsh girl named Sara Jacobs.   [   ]

3. Mika and Angela are both concerned about the problem of   [   ]
   homelessness but are not sure how to help.

Discussion ///

1. Based on the reading passage, do you think the addition of references and examples from the Great Famine add to the story of Anna O'Donnell? Do you think the movie would be different without this? If possible, watch *The Wonder* and then discuss.

2. Listen to the dialogue again. Mika says, 'We should still try to help, but I'm not sure how is best'. What do you think individuals can do when faced with a very large problem? Do you think helping even in a small way is meaningful?

Homework/Research ///

Research online to find out more about the causes and effects of the Great Famine. If possible, watch some movies about the Great Famine, such as:

• *The Great Irish Famine* (1996)
• *Ireland's Great Hunger and the Irish Diaspora* (2015)
• *Black '47* (2018)
• *Arracht* (2019)

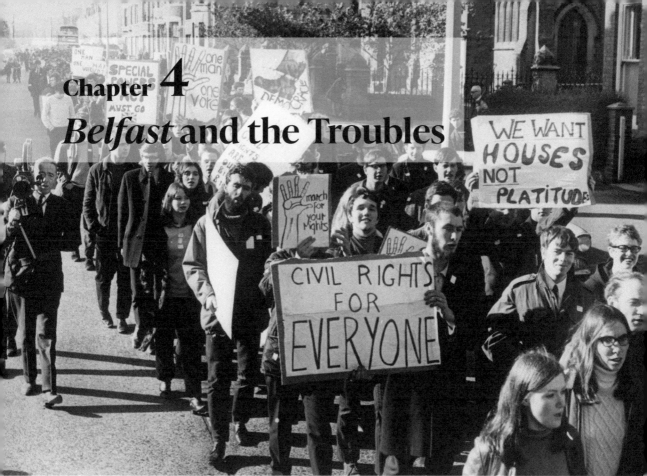

Chapter 4
Belfast and the Troubles

©IWM. Civil Unrest in Northern Ireland 1968-1969: Students at Belfast University carrying banners proclaiming 'Civil rights for everyone', the 'Special Powers Act Must Go', and 'We want Houses Not Platitudes', march through Belfast to the City Hall in October 1968.

Warming-Up Activities

1. Brainstorming on the Topic

イングランドとアイルランドの関係について何を知っているだろう？　どうしてアイルランドはアイルランド共和国と北アイルランドに分かれているのだろう？　アイルランドで 'the Troubles'（常に大文字）で言えば、何を指すのだろう？

2. Vocabulary

☐ **sectarian** 形 分派の、宗派の、派閥的な

☐ **inequality** 名 不平等（対 **equality**）

☐ **confrontation** 名 対決、衝突

☐ **riot** 自動 暴動を起こす 名 暴動

☐ **apolitical** 形 政治に無関心な

☐ **sufficiently** 副 充分に（形 **sufficient**）

☐ **conform** 自動（to...）〜に従う、順応する

☐ **opt** 自動（for...）〜を選択する、（**to do**）〜する

☐ **coherent** 形 首尾一貫した、統一性のある

☐ **dedication** 名 献身、献呈

🔊 Audio 1-08

The origins of the thirty years of sectarian conflict in Northern Ireland, generally referred to as simply 'the Troubles', can be traced back
5 to the civil rights demonstrations and protests in the late 1960s. The Northern Ireland Civil Rights Association (NICRA) held its first

protest march on 24 August 1968 to call attention to the inequality (especially for
10 Catholic residents) in jobs, housing, education and political representation. The march was cut short, though, when police stopped the marchers from entering a town where a Protestant counter-protest was waiting for them. However, a second march held on 5 October 1968 in Derry ended with the police from the Royal Ulster Constabulary (RUC) charging and beating the protesters with batons. All
15 of which was caught on camera and broadcast on television.

Many historians, though, look to the events of August 1969 as the true beginning of the Troubles. In what became known as 'the Battle of the Bogside', on 12 August a pro-British loyalist parade in Derry passed through the Catholic area of Bogside resulting in a violent confrontation lasting three days with rioting
20 in Belfast which left 1,500 homes in Catholic neighbourhoods destroyed. On 14 August, with the situation in Northern Ireland out of control, the British government sent in troops to restore order. They would remain in Northern Ireland for the next 38 years.

It should come as no surprise, then, when Kenneth Branagh begins *Belfast*
25 with the on-screen text: '15th August, 1969'. *Belfast*, released in 2021, is the latest in a long line of films set in Northern Ireland during the Troubles, but it is not a film from which a viewer will leave well informed about the history and politics of the Troubles. Donald Clarke, reviewing the movie in *The Irish Times*, describes *Belfast* as being 'aggressively apolitical' and 'will do little to educate the wider
30 world about the inequalities that fertilised the coming violence'. Peter Bradshaw in *The Guardian* predicts that some viewers may feel that the movie 'does not sufficiently conform to the template of political anger and despair considered

appropriate for dramas about Northern Ireland and the Troubles'.

Branagh, though, opts for telling a more personal story: an unapologetically nostalgic look back at his own childhood in Belfast before his family immigrated 35

Belfast (Universal Pictures, 2022)

to England. The family consists of nine-year-old Buddy as the stand-in for Branagh, plus his mother and father, grandparents and older brother, Will. In the opening scene, 40 Buddy is running and playing in the street. Suddenly, shouting is heard, and a rioting mob rounds the corner, throwing rocks and petrol bombs, blowing up a car and burning out 45 the homes of Catholic residents in this mixed Protestant/Catholic neighbourhood. As described above, what Buddy witnesses is part of the anti-Catholic 'Battle of the Bogside' riots. Buddy, of course, knows nothing of the history and politics of the Troubles. That's the point. The audience is meant to experience the Troubles as Buddy does: random scenes of violence, bits of overheard conversation from 50 adults, nothing fully coherent and understandable. As a personal story, the movie focuses on the parents' difficult decision of whether to leave Belfast, their only home, or risk the safety of their family.

Belfast ends with another on-screen text: 'For the ones who stayed. For the ones who left. And for all those who were lost forever.' Between the date at the 55 beginning of the film and the dedication at the end is the space where the political story exists. This is where we know what the characters don't know. We know what is coming: the violence and bloodshed resulting in more than 3,700 deaths during the thirty years of the Troubles.

NOTES

ll. 6-8: **The Northern Ireland Civil Rights Association (NICRA)** 北アイルランド公民権協会
ll. 13-14: **the Royal Ulster Constabulary (RUC)** 王立アルスター警察隊
l. 17: **the Battle of the Bogside** ボグサイドの戦い（デリー市のボグサイド地区で起こった衝突）
l. 18: **loyalist** 名 ロイヤリスト（イギリス本国との分離に反対する北アイルランド住民）
l. 30: **fertilised > fertilise, -ize** 他動 ～を肥沃にする、～の発達を促す
l. 32: **template** 名 テンプレート、雛形、モデル
l. 34: **unapologetically** 副 弁解しようともせずに、堂々と

1. According to the passage,

   (A) the second civil rights march in 1968 was much more violent than the first.

   (B) the first civil rights march in 1968 was much more violent than the second.

   (C) both civil rights marches in 1968 were televised.

   (D) both civil rights marches in 1968 took place on the same day in different towns.

2. During the 'Battle of the Bogside', 1,500 homes in Catholic neighbourhoods in Belfast were destroyed by

   (A) British troops.

   (B) loyalists.

   (C) the NICRA.

   (D) historians.

3. In paragraph 3, Donald Clarke implies that the violent events of the Troubles were a result of

   (A) the release of *Belfast* in 2021.

   (B) being aggressively apolitical.

   (C) people not being well informed.

   (D) the inequalities in Northern Ireland.

4. In paragraph 3, Peter Bradshaw implies that some viewers of *Belfast*

   (A) will want to see more anger and despair about the Troubles.

   (B) will consider the movie to be an appropriate drama about Northern Ireland.

   (C) will leave the movie feeling well informed.

   (D) will agree with his review of the movie rather than Donald Clarke's.

5.–7. Complete the summary of paragraph 4 below. Choose one word only from the passage for each answer.

Nine-year-old Buddy serves as a **5.**_____ for Kenneth Branagh in *Belfast*. And unlike the adult Branagh, Buddy knows **6.**_____ about the politics and history of the Troubles. As a director, Branagh wants the audience to **7.**_____ the events in the movie as Buddy does.

Listening Comprehension ///

🔊 **Audio 1-09**

Listen to the conversation between Ben and Motoki after watching Belfast. Answer whether the following statements are **true** or **false**.

1. Motoki was not surprised by the ending of the movie.   [   ]

2. Motoki was very impressed with Caitríona Balfe's   [   ]
   performance in the movie.

3. Granny is a very minor character with little screen time.   [   ]

1. Discuss the ending on-screen text: 'For the ones who stayed. For the ones who left. And for all those who were lost forever.'

2. For Kenneth Branagh, leaving Ireland at the age of nine and immigrating to England dramatically changed his life. What events in your life so far (though perhaps not so dramatic) do you think you will look back on as having changed your life?

Homework/Research ////

1. Watch *Belfast* and be prepared to discuss in class.

2. Choose an event, topic or person related to the Troubles to research and report on in class. Some possible choices:

Bloody Sunday

The Bloody Sunday Inquiry

The Omagh bombing

The Provisional Irish Republican Army (IRA)

The Royal Ulster Constabulary (RUC)

The Maze Prison Hunger Strikes

Bobby Sands

Gerry Adams

The Belfast (Good Friday) Agreement

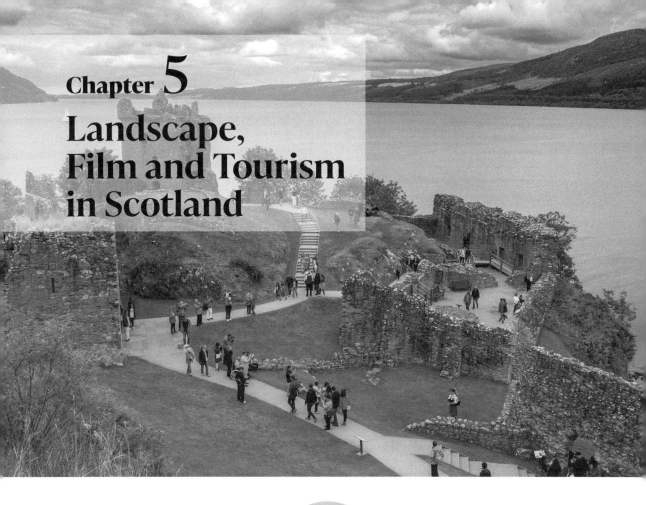

Chapter 5
Landscape, Film and Tourism in Scotland

Warming-Up Activities

1. Brainstorming on the Topic

人はどうして旅行に出るのだろう？　よく選ばれる旅行先にはどんな魅力があるのだろう？　観光は国の経済に重要な貢献をしているのだろうか？　以下の Vocabulary から二つ以上の語を選んでブレインストーミングをし、ディスカッションしてみよう。

2. Vocabulary

- ☐ medieval 形 中世の（cf. ancient 古代の）
- ☐ stunning 形 驚くべき、息をのむほど美しい
- ☐ landscape 名 風景
- ☐ heritage site 名 ヘリテージ・サイト（史跡）
- ☐ spectacular 形 壮観の、見世物的な

- ☐ scenery 名 風景
- ☐ strategy 名 戦略
- ☐ cliché 名 決まり文句、月並みな主題
- ☐ anticipate 他動 ～を予想する、予期する
- ☐ resilience 自動 回復力、レジリエンス

If you love Pixar animations, you have probably seen 2012's *Brave*. Set in Scotland during medieval times, it's the story of a rebellious, red-headed heroine named Merida. Then again, maybe not. The film got bland reviews and a mere two or three stars. Reviewers agreed, however, on the film's stunning digital
⁵ rendering of Highland landscapes and heritage sites. The Scottish landscape has, in fact, long been a favourite of filmmakers in search of spectacular natural scenery and historic settings. In the case of *Brave*, Scotland's national tourist agency, VisitScotland, took the unprecedented step of partnering with Pixar on the production and investing seven-million pounds on a global *Brave*-themed
¹⁰ Discover Scotland campaign. In 2022, VisitScotland released *Set in Scotland*, a guide to locations featured in global blockbusters—from Marvel to Harry Potter to James Bond. Clearly, film and landscape are an important mix in Scotland's tourism strategy.

The 1954 American film classic *Brigadoon* popularised many of Scotland's
¹⁵ 'invented' traditions and images—tartans, bagpipes, misty valleys. Based on a 1947 Broadway musical, the film is about two American hunters who, while hiking through the Highlands, discover a magical village that appears for only one day every one hundred years. For many Scots, the film presents all the clichés one would expect from Hollywood. For others, the film captures something
²⁰ essentially Scottish. Scotland's proud history, seen in *Culloden* (1964), *Mary, Queen of Scots* (1971), *Highlander* (1986), *Rob Roy* (1995), *Outlaw King* (2018) and *Robert the Bruce* (2019), has also contributed to tourism. 1995's *Braveheart*, a violent American epic about Scotland's 13th century rebellion against English rule alerted the industry to the promotional potential of film. Aside from the gory
²⁵ battles, there is plenty of stunning landscape to see—never mind that many scenes were shot in Ireland to save costs. The film's release coincided with deregulation of the airline industry and the availability of low-cost flights into Scotland. From that point, the film and tourism strategy took off, so to speak.

Today, tourism is a major part of Scotland's economy, contributing about
³⁰ six billion pounds, or 5% of GDP annually. With approximately 14,000 tourism-related businesses nationwide, it plays an important role in sustaining rural and urban economies. Landscape is the main attraction. 2015 and 2016 visitor surveys

found that in all categories—native Scots, UK visitors, European tourists, first-time visitors, returning visitors—'scenery and landscape' topped the lists. Among Europeans, the figure was 71%; for first-time visitors, almost 60%. The COVID 35 pandemic shifted motives for travel and promotion as people looked for ways to restore their mental health after lockdown. More than 50% wanted to connect with nature, and a full 80% of 2021 visitors chose the countryside. Rural coastlines and islands topped the list at 40%, countryside and village at 37%, mountains or hills at 32%. Recent promotional campaigns present Scotland as an 'emotional 40 destination', its landscapes offering awe, mysticism and passion, involvement and escape.

Edie (2017) celebrates the healing power of landscape, anticipating many of the post-COVID trends in tourism. Edith Moore is an 83-year-old, recently widowed English woman who journeys to Inverness in the Scottish Highlands to 45 climb Suilven. After a life of sacrifice to an abusive husband and now facing her final years in a retirement home, Edie decides to take control and keep a promise she made to her father to climb the mountain. In Lochinver, she meets Jonny, a young local who, along with his partner Fiona, has borrowed heavily to expand their camping business. In need of money, Jonny becomes Edie's trainer and 50 guide—and outfits her in new camping gear. Edie, a former camping enthusiast, vows to quit a number of times before she makes the journey to the summit. Resilience, VisitScotland's research tells us, is one of the benefits of travel. The film teaches us that it is never too late to challenge ourselves.

NOTES

l. 1: **Pixar** ピクサー (アメリカ合衆国のアニメーション制作会社)
l. 3: **bland** 形 淡泊な、味気のない
l. 5: **Highland** ハイランド (スコットランドは南部のローランドと北部のハイランドに分かれる)
l. 8: **unprecedented** 形 前例のない
l. 11: **blockbusters > blockbuster** 名 超大作、大ヒット作
l. 11: **Marvel** マーヴェル (アメリカ合衆国の漫画出版社)
l. 15: **tartans > tartan** 名 タータンチェック (の毛織物) (英語では 'tartan check' とは言わないので注意)
l. 24: **gory** 形 血みどろの、残虐な
l. 26: **deregulation** 名 規制撤廃、規制緩和
l. 30: **GDP** 国内総生産 (=gross domestic product)
l. 35: **COVID** 新型コロナウイルス感染症
l. 41: **awe** 名 畏怖
l. 41: **mysticism** 名 神秘主義、神秘体験
l. 51: **outfits > outfit** 他動 ～に供給する、支度する (ここでは名詞ではないので注意)

1. According to the passage, promotion of travel to Scotland changed significantly after the COVID pandemic in response to

    (A) low-cost flights into the country.

    (B) a shortage of staff in the hospitality sector.

    (C) mental health impacts.

    (D) tourists' preference for rural sightseeing.

2.–6. Do the following statements agree with the information given in the passage? Write **true** (the statement agrees with the information), **false** (the statement contradicts the information) or **not given** (there is no information on this).

2. Scotland's tourist office partnered with Pixar on production and promotion of *Braveheart*.

3. International visits to Scotland dropped by about eighty-six percent during the COVID pandemic.

4. Europeans were most likely to choose 'scenery and landscape' as the reason for visiting Scotland.

5. According to the 2016 survey, movies and films inspired nine percent of foreign, especially American, visitors to Scotland. *Braveheart* topped the list of films.

6. Over 80% of travellers were seeking relief from the effects of lockdown.

7. In paragraph 3, all of the following statements are true EXCEPT:

(A) About 60% of those coming to Scotland for the first time were interested in experiencing landscape.

(B) Tourism makes a significant contribution to Scotland's economy.

(C) Mountains or hills attracted roughly half of those who visited rural areas.

(D) Tourism helps sustain livelihoods in the city as well as the countryside.

Listening Comprehension

🔊 Audio 1-11

Listen to the commentary on the film *Edie*. Answer whether the following statements are **true** or **false**.

1. The commentator thinks *Edie* was a tedious film.   [   ]

2. The commentator rejects criticism of the relationship between characters in the film.   [   ]

3. The commentator enjoyed the natural landscapes in the film but couldn't help feeling that the film had a strong intention to promote tourism.   [   ]

Discussion ////

'Therapeutic landscape' is a concept introduced by health geographer Wilbert Gesler. According to Gesler, a therapeutic landscape or space is an area 'where the physical and built environments, social conditions and human perceptions combine to produce an atmosphere which is conducive to healing'. Based on what you have read and on your own experience, discuss how landscapes and other kinds of spaces can benefit people emotionally, mentally and physically.

Homework/Research ////

1. Choose a place that you have visited and discuss it as a therapeutic landscape or therapeutic space. What emotions did you experience in this place? How did it benefit you? Alternatively, choose a tourist site in your home country that could be considered a therapeutic space. How do people use it? What emotional, mental or physical benefits do they receive?

2. Download the *Set in Scotland* guidebook from the VisitScotland homepage:

 https://www.visitscotland.com/ebrochures/en/set-in-scotland.pdf

Work with group members to plan a three-day tour of your favourite Scottish filming locations. Research the background to each location and then discuss what qualities the landscapes and heritage sites lend to each film. Present your travel plan and research to the class.

Chapter **6**
The Legacy of the Beatles

1. Brainstorming on the Topic

ビートルズについてどんなことを知っているだろう？　ポピュラーミュージックやポピュ
ラーカルチャーにおいてどれほど重要な役割を果たしているだろう？　以下の Vocabulary
から二つ以上の語を選んでブレインストーミングをし、ディスカッションしてみよう。

2. Vocabulary

□ **legacy** 名 遺産
□ **track** 名 (アルバム中の)曲
□ **speculate** 自動 思索する、(that…と)憶測する
□ **feat** 名 手柄、偉業
□ **restoration** 名 回復、修復(cf. restore)

□ **alternate** 形 交互の、既存のものに代わる
□ **affecting** 形 感動的な
□ **speechless** 形 唖然とした、言葉が出せない
□ **reconstruct** 他動 ～を復元する、再現する
□ **rendition** 名 演奏

🔊 Audio 1-12

On 12 June 2023, Sir Paul McCartney announced the release of the last Beatles record, some fifty years after the band broke up. Excitement turned to controversy as McCartney revealed that AI was used to complete the song. The track was not generated by AI as many fans thought. Rather, AI-powered software

5 was used to extract a vocal of John Lennon from a song called 'Now and Then', which he had recorded at his home in New York City in the late 1970s, a few years before he was killed. The three surviving Beatles, Paul, George Harrison and Ringo Starr, met in 1995 to work on a number of Lennon's home recordings, but 'Now and Then' had to wait almost twenty more years for a little help from

10 AI technology. Featuring contributions from all of the Beatles, 'Now and Then' was released on 2 November 2023 and quickly shot to number one in the UK, a fitting capstone to the band's legacy. In 2022, at the Glastonbury Festival, the same technology made it possible for McCartney to perform a video duet with Lennon using video from the Beatles' famous rooftop concert in 1969. Film

15 director Peter Jackson was behind both technological feats thanks to his work on the 2021 documentary *The Beatles: Get Back*, which looks in on the rehearsal and recording sessions for the *Let It Be* album and documentary (1970). For the eight-hour film, Jackson used AI to restore the murky video and poor sound quality, while also pulling out conversations of people in the studio. For fans, the film is

20 not just a restoration; it's a revelation of the creative process and personalities of John, Paul, George and Ringo. The film dispels the long-held opinion that the band were angry and miserable during these sessions. Of course, tensions do arise. However, the film shows the

25 Beatles as friends, having fun and joyously making music together. McCartney even jokes about the break-up myth: 'It's going to be such an incredible, comical thing in 50 years' time. "They broke up 'cause Yoko sat on an amp"'.

Yesterday (US vinyl picture sleeve, 1965)

30 The 2019 film *Yesterday*, directed by Danny Boyle, honours the Beatles' legacy in a much different way, inviting us to imagine a world where the Fab Four never came together. Jack Malik is a struggling singer-songwriter who is

about to give up his dream when a mysterious global blackout transports him to an alternate reality without the Beatles. This world also lacks cigarettes and Coca Cola, and there's no Oasis or Harry Potter—odd choices. Odd, too, that the film pays no attention to how the social and political order might be different. Fair enough, it's a film about music. But, of course, it is hard to imagine a world without the Beatles where pop music is not profoundly different. So what is the intent of the film? Some of the most affecting moments come when Jack performs a song to a small circle of listeners. Early on, Jack is presented with a new guitar and launches into 'Yesterday', leaving his friends glassy-eyed and speechless. 'What the hell was that?' his manager Ellie asks. 'That was one of the most beautiful songs I've ever heard,' says another. The group's ignorance of the Beatles makes Jack think they are playing a joke on him, but after a frantic Google search, he realises the truth and sets out to restart his career, spending hours trying to reconstruct the words and music of the Beatles' songs. Later, the songs—posted online—come to the notice of superstar Ed Sheeran, who invites Jack to join him on tour. During one of their Russian concerts, Sheeran challenges Jack to a song-writing competition. Jack's rendition of 'The Long and Winding Road' silences the room, and a humbled Sheeran calls himself Salieri to Malik's Mozart.

But the film's most affecting moment is not about music at all. At the concert launching Jack's debut album, a man and woman confront Jack. Jack fears that he will be exposed, but they only wish to thank him for bringing the Beatle's music into the world. Before leaving, they give Jack a slip of paper. We see Jack arriving at a seaside cottage. Jack knocks. John Lennon's aged face appears at the door. It's a moment that seems to have left most audiences in tears. This moment—and the new song, McCartney's 2022 duet—reminds us how much John Lennon continues to loom large in the Beatles' legacy.

NOTES

l. 18: **murky** 形 陰気な、不明瞭な
l. 21: **dispels > dispel** 他動 〜を追い散らす、消散させる
ll. 31-32: **the Fab Four = the Fabulous Four = the Beatles**
l. 33: **blackout** 名 停電
l. 33: **transports > transport** 他動 〜を移動させる、いざなう
l. 41: **launches into > launch into** 〜に乗り出す
l. 41: **glassy-eyed** 形 ぼんやりとした (目つきの)
l. 44: **frantic** 形 半狂乱の
l. 58: **loom large** 大きく立ちはだかる

1. McCartney's announcement of a new Beatles song created controversy because
   (A) it was more than fifty years since the band broke up.
   (B) John Lennon was murdered in New York City in 1980.
   (C) fans believed that AI was used to create the song.
   (D) fans were told that AI-based machine learning was used to improve the track.

2. The author says that *Get Back*
   (A) shows the Beatles were angry and miserable during this final period of their career.
   (B) gives insight into the character of each of the Beatles and the way they wrote their songs.
   (C) reveals Yoko Ono's role in the break-up of the Beatles.
   (D) is, at almost eight hours, too long for most casual Beatles fans.

3. In paragraph 2, the author finds it strange that the film *Yesterday*
   (A) features a number of acoustic performances.
   (B) includes Ed Sheeran.
   (C) tries to imagine world without the Beatles.
   (D) does not examine other ways the world might be different.

4.–7. Complete the summary of paragraph one below. Choose one word only from the passage for each answer.

Film-maker Peter Jackson used AI-based technology to help create a new **4.**_____ by the Beatles. He also made it possible for McCartney to perform a **5.**_____ with John Lennon on stage. In the **6.**_____ film *Get Back* the same technology was used to **7.**_____ sound and video from the 1969 recording sessions for the *Let It Be* album and film.

Listening Comprehension ////

🔊 Audio 1-13

Listen to the commentary on the film *Yesterday*. Answer whether the following statements are **true** or **false**.

1. The commentator discusses his favourite scene in the film. [　　]

2. The commentator thinks the scene gives insight into Ellie's character. [　　]

3. The commentator thinks the film thoroughly explores the Beatles' cultural impact. [　　]

How do you think AI will affect music? Do artists need to protect themselves from misuse and copying by AI? Have you listened to AI versions of songs by your favourite artists? What do you think of the AI versions?

Homework/Research ////

1. Investigate further the final years of the Beatles. What tensions were in the band? Why did they break up?

2. Research the Beatles' influence on pop music by choosing one or two groups from the 1960s or one or more recent artists who have been influenced by them.

3. The American music magazine *Rolling Stone* has called 'Now and Then' the 'world's greatest musical love story'. Investigate the making of the song, including the special significance it seems to hold for Paul McCartney.

Chapter 7
Friends
—Real, Virtual, Artificial

1. Brainstorming on the Topic

ソーシャルメディア(SNS)や人工知能(AI)について知っていることを挙げてみよう。これらの技術はどのように人々の関係を変えたのだろうか。日本とイギリスで違いはあるのだろうか。それとも同じ問題に直面しているのだろうか。

2. Vocabulary

☐ **address** 他動 ～に取り組む

☐ **cyberbullying** 名 ネットいじめ

☐ **permission** 名 許可

☐ **well-being** 名 幸福、福利

☐ **interpersonal** 形 対人の

☐ **interact** 自動 (with...と) 交流する

☐ **compensate** 自動 (for...の) 埋め合わせをする

☐ **socialise, -ize** 自動 友達づきあいする

☐ **allegory** 名 寓意、寓話、アレゴリー

☐ **plagiarism** 名 剽窃 (plagiarise, -ize 他動 剽窃する)

Audio 1-14

Technology has changed our social lives. Online communication apps and social media have made it easier to stay connected with friends all the time and have even changed the
5 definition of 'friendship'. The statistics show that as of 2023, 96% of children aged 16–17 in Britain have a smartphone, and more than half of children over seven years old have mobile devices. Whenever you have something to tell your friends, all you have to do is grab your smartphone and message them. More than 40 million
10 people exchange messages, share photos and videos, and make voice and video calls on WhatsApp, the most popular social media platform in the UK. Who are your 'friends' anyway? On Facebook, you can easily *friend* someone you have never met in person. You can follow anyone on X or Instagram. Young people are less likely to hesitate to find friends online—'virtual friends'—or *defriend* them
15 whenever they find it right.

We do not know how we should handle this new situation yet. Critics have constantly warned us of the dangers of social media and online communication. Some have voiced security concerns, and others have addressed issues such as mental health and crime. Cyberbullying, for example, has posed a new challenge.
20 Some victims receive mean messages, and others see unflattering or inappropriate pictures of them posted or shared without permission. In 2017, the BBC's *Newsline* covered an interview with a mother. She was surprised that police officers came along and arrested her 14-year-old daughter for sending her friend a hurtful message asking her to self-harm and consider suicide. She was shocked at the ease
25 with which her daughter composed such a message and pressed the 'Send' button without any consideration of the consequences. Now, people can harass others without even looking at their faces.

Of course, it is not very wise to attack social media unfairly. A team of researchers led by Rebecca Anthony of Cardiff University discovered that *some*
30 use of social media leads to higher mental well-being of students aged 11–16. In an article published in *Child and Adolescent Mental Health*, they argue that students' quality of life improves if they frequently communicate online with their best

friends and larger friendship groups. Their findings also suggest a high frequency of communication with virtual friends badly affects their mental well-being. Online friends cannot replace offline friends. The new means of communication 35 can strengthen existing interpersonal relationships and yet cannot always relieve our loneliness. After all, technology simply amplifies what is already there: friendship, anxiety and hatred.

We may be moving into a new phase. Besides virtual friends, we may have *artificial* friends soon. In 2022–23, we witnessed 40 breakthroughs in generative AI (artificial intelligence). AI chatbots like OpenAI's ChatGPT can interact with users much the same way as humans. What if AI begins to act as your friend? British novelist Kazuo Ishiguro's *Klara and the Sun* (2021) gives us a glimpse of a dystopian future. 45 As schooling is entirely online, wealthy parents purchase 'AFs'—'Artificial Friends', or AI-equipped androids— to compensate for their children's limited opportunities to socialise with others. <u>Predictably</u>, children become

Klara and the Sun (Faber and Faber, 2021)

impertinent and inconsiderate. They pick on weaker children—humans or 50 AFs—when they are with their peers. Adults have problems, too. Chrissie purchases Klara, an AF, hoping that she can replace her sick daughter, Josie, who she believes will die soon. Meanwhile, Klara has the now rare ability to perceive pain in others and finally sacrifices herself to save the sick girl. Towards the end, we see Klara dumped in a recycling facility. Friends are literally disposable. 55 Is it really a dystopian future? Or is it an allegory of what is happening now?

NOTES

l. 5: **statistics** 名 統計
l. 11: **WhatsApp** ワッツアップ
l. 12: **Facebook** フェイスブック
l. 13: **X** X (2023年7月にツイッターから改称したSNS)
l. 13: **Instagram** インスタグラム
l. 20: **unflattering** 形 写りの悪い
l. 29: **Cardiff** カーディフ (ウェールズの都市)
l. 37: **amplifies > amplify** 他動 ～を増幅する
l. 41: **breakthroughs > breakthrough** 名 躍進、ブレイクスルー
l. 41: **generative AI** 生成AI
l. 42: **chatbots > chatbot** 名 チャットボット
l. 45: **dystopian** 形 ディストピア的な、悪夢のような
l. 55: **disposable** 形 使い捨ての

1. It can be inferred from paragraph 1 that before the arrival of online communication apps and social media, it was

   (A) not as common to make friends with people you had never seen face-to-face as it is now.

   (B) extremely rare for parents to allow children to have smartphones or other mobile devices.

   (C) easy to know what your friends were doing even when you were not with them.

   (D) impossible to make friends with someone you had never seen face-to-face.

2. In paragraph 2, the author cites the BBC's *Newsline* to

   (A) provide the potential legal consequences of hurtful messages.

   (B) illustrate how easily hurtful messages can be transmitted.

   (C) highlight the need for stricter parental control of social media usage.

   (D) discuss the effects of cyberbullying and online harassment on victims.

3. According to paragraph 3, a team of researchers found out that

   (A) regular communication with online friends improves students' mental well-being.

   (B) all types of online communication have a positive effect on students' mental well-being.

   (C) students who interact well with offline and online friends have higher mental well-being.

   (D) students who only interact with online friends are likely to suffer lower mental well-being.

4. In paragraph 4, the author uses the word Predictably because lack of socialisation

   (A) often makes children selfish and rude.

   (B) usually aggravates children's loneliness.

(C) rarely affects children's interpersonal skills.

(D) always damages children's mental wellbeing.

5. Which of the following statements can be inferred from paragraph 4?

(A) AI chatbots can enhance our ability to socialise with humans.

(B) The right use of AI is an effective solution to children's limited socialisation.

(C) AI can aggravate the problems for which humans are responsible.

(D) AI merely produces negative consequences and creates a dystopian society.

6.–7. Complete the note below. Use one word only from the passage for the answer.

By using apps like WhatsApp, you can cement 6._____ relationships you already have offline. But if you only talk with *virtual* friends, you may not be able to get over your 7._____.

Listening Comprehension ///

Audio 1-15

Listen to the conversation between two university lecturers, Alex and Ken, about a topic covered in the reading passage. Answer whether the following statements are **true** or **false**.

1. Alex was surprised to know AI text generators commit plagiarism.   [   ]

2. Ken finds the recreational or educational use of AI problematic.   [   ]

3. According Oscar Wilde, it is selfish to think and act for yourself.   [   ]

Discussion

1. How do you find Rebecca Anthony and her team's findings? Do you agree or disagree? Use specific reasons and examples to support your view.

2. Listen to the dialogue again. What do you think of the potential effects of generative AI on children? How do you think we can avoid the worst scenario mentioned in the conversation?

Homework/Research

1. Conduct a structured or semi-structured interview with three people of different social groups (e.g. age, gender, profession, nationality) about online communication and social media. Make sure to get their consent and respect their privacy. Create a poster summing up your research.

2. Input a couple of questions into an AI text generator (e.g. ChatGPT), or ask your teacher to do it. Evaluate the program's responses in groups and find out its capabilities and limitations.

Chapter **8**

'Your Very Good Health': The National Health Service in Crisis

1. Brainstorming on the Topic

日本の健康保険制度についてどんなことを知っているだろう？　あるいは、アメリカ合衆国やイギリスについてはどうだろう？　公的健康保険サービスよりも私企業の有料サービスのほうが効率的だろうか。以下の Vocabulary から二つ以上の語を選んでブレインストーミングをし、ディスカッションしてみよう。

2. Vocabulary

- ☐ transformation 名 変容、変形
- ☐ public healthcare 公的健康保険
- ☐ legislation 名 立法、法律
- ☐ market-oriented 形 市場志向の
- ☐ bureaucracy 名 官僚主義、書類手続き
- ☐ benefit 名 恩恵、給付
- ☐ socialised medicine, -ized — 社会主義的な医療
- ☐ frontline 名 最前線、第一線
- ☐ ideological 形 イデオロギーの(名 ideology)
- ☐ privatisation, -ization 名 民営化(形 private)

The opening ceremony of the 30th Olympic Games in London in 2012 was a spectacular celebration of Great Britain. The four-hour extravaganza, directed by filmmaker Danny Boyle, told the story of England's transformation from 'a green and pleasant land' through its industrialisation to the post-imperial glory of
5 cultural icons such as the Beatles, James Bond, Mr Bean, Mary Poppins and punk rock. One of the highlights was Boyle's loving tribute to the National Health Service (NHS) and the Great Ormond Street Hospital, which featured 1,800 dancers and nurses, a host of children and more than 300 beds. Soon after the games, revelations of political interference—attempts to cut the NHS sequence—fuelled suspicion
10 about the government's designs on the world's first public healthcare system. In the lead-up to the Olympics, parliament debated the Health and Social Care Act, a landmark piece of legislation that dissolved the responsibility of the Secretary of State to provide healthcare for all citizens and introduced a private, market-oriented bureaucracy. 2012 was indeed a fateful year for healthcare in the UK.

15 The NHS was launched in 1948 with a promotional campaign by the new Central Information Office. 'Charley, Your Very Good Health', an animation created for the launch, shows the government hard at work convincing a sceptical public of the benefits of socialised medicine. Medical dramas became a staple of television entertainment and played an important role in shaping attitudes towards
20 the healthcare system. *Emergency Ward 10* (1957–1967) carried on efforts to build trust in modern medicine. Since then, TV dramas and comedies featuring doctors and their practices, midwives, nurses and paramedics, emergency departments and care homes have attracted large audiences. *Casualty*, which first aired on the BBC in 1986, is the longest running medical drama series in the world, with more
25 than 1,200 episodes and a spin-off called *Holby City* (1999-2022). Creators Paul Unwin and Jeremy Brock conceived the original series, set in an Accident and Emergency department of a Bristol hospital, as an exploration of the 'frontline' of the NHS and of British society. Featuring a diverse cast, the series has often dealt with controversial issues, from HIV/AIDS to healthcare funding cuts. Indeed,
30 the creators wanted to draw the public into 'the battle for the soul of the NHS', in the face of prime minister Margaret Thatcher's attacks on public healthcare. Hospital closures, waiting lists, shortages of staff and resources, conflicts between

medical staff and management about budgets have, among many other themes, been explored through the years.

The political and ideological context for the NHS crisis and calls to action 35 are presented in *Under the Knife* (2019), *The Great NHS Heist* (2019) and *The Dirty War on the NHS* (2019). These documentaries remind Britons of the transformation from a patchwork of paid healthcare before WWII to free, socialised medicine after. They also chronicle the political battles of the 1970s, 80s and 90s leading to the current crisis. Before Thatcher took office, plans were being made to return 40 the NHS to the private sector by 'stealth'. By the late 80s, a report entitled 'Britain's Biggest Enterprise' made clear the profit motive for 'reform'. Privatisation gained momentum in the 1990s under the New Labour government of Tony Blair. An American model of for-profit healthcare has advanced steadily thanks to the efforts of think tanks, lobbies, management consultancies, private corporations 45 and MPs. The COVID pandemic, which began in 2020 and claimed more than 200,000 lives in the UK, exposed the many problems of an underfunded NHS. A six-week inquiry found austerity and Brexit to be prime factors in the failure. New 'reform' legislation, the 2022 Health and Care Act, will further fragment the NHS and promote privatisation, say critics. As the NHS celebrated 75 years of 50 service in 2023, a new fifteen-year, £2.4 billion plan to 'train, retain and reform' was announced by PM Rishi Sunak. Is the NHS on the road to recovery?

NOTES

l. 2: **extravaganza** 名 狂想曲、豪華絢爛な催し

ll. 3-4: **'a green and pleasant land'** 愛国歌にもなっている、ロマン派の詩人ウィリアム・ブレイクの「エルサレム」の一節 'In England's green and pleasant land' (イングランドの清純なる緑野に)) から

l. 4: **industrialisation, -ization** 名 工業化、産業化

l. 7: **the Great Ormond Street Hospital** グレート・オーモンド・ストリート病院(ロンドンの小児病院)

ll. 12-13: **the Secretary of the State** 閣内大臣 (内務大臣、国防大臣など)

ll. 15-16: **the Central Information Office** 中央情報局

l. 22: **midwives > midwife** 名 助産師

l. 22: **paramedics > paramedic** 名 医療補助者、救急医療士

l. 32: **closures > closure** 名 閉鎖

l. 43: **New Labour** ニュー・レイバー

l. 45: **think tanks > think tank** シンクタンク

l. 45: **lobbies > lobby** 名 ロビー、圧力団体

1.–5. Do the following statements agree with the information given in the passage? Write **true** (the statement agrees with the information), **false** (the statement contradicts the information) or **not given** (there is no information on this).

1. A number of powerful groups have pushed Britain to adopt an American model of private healthcare.

2. In the 1990s, *Casualty* had a weekly average of 14 million viewers.

3. The New Labour government published its plan to privatise the NHS in the 1980s.

4. After the Olympic games, the Health and Social Care Act was debated in parliament.

5. Private outsourcing of PPE and shortages of staff and beds were some of the problems experienced during the COVID pandemic.

6. Expanded privatisation
   (A) is considered essential to preserving the NHS.
   (B) was debated by parliament in 2012.
   (C) was rejected by the New Labour government in the 1990s.
   (D) is one of the criticisms of the 2022 Health and Care Act.

7. According to the passage, the COVID pandemic
   (A) revealed the weaknesses of the NHS.
   (B) has been blamed on austerity and Brexit.
   (C) forced many nurses and doctors to leave the NHS.
   (D) resulted in the deaths of almost two-hundred thousand people across Europe.

Listening Comprehension ////

🔊 Audio 1-17

Listen to the lecture excerpt on global trends in healthcare. Make notes and answer whether the following statements agree with the information given in the lecture. Write **true** (the statement agrees with the information), **false** (the statement contradicts the information) or **not given** (there is no information on this).

1. Private healthcare is increasing across the industrialised world.   [   ]

2. One common trend is the contracting of privately owned   [   ]
   services to the public system.

3. Neoliberalism promotes increases in spending on public   [   ]
   healthcare and social services.

1. Based on what you have read and heard, do you think it is inevitable that healthcare will become more privatised in the future—in Japan and around the world?

2. Debate the following statement with classmates, taking pro or con (for or against) positions: Individuals make choices about lifestyle (diet, exercise, smoking, consumption of alcohol) that affect their health; therefore, healthcare costs should be borne by individuals, not by society.

Homework/Research ////

1. Visit the website for the NHS Support Federation <https://nhscampaign.org/> or Keep Our NHS Public <https://keepournhspublic.com/>. Research and report to the class on one or more issues facing the NHS.

NHS Support Federation   Keep Our NHS Public

2. How does Japan rank globally in terms of health and healthcare? Investigate one or more issues in regard to Japan's healthcare system and the policies that regulate it.

Chapter 9
'Keep Calm and Carry On': Two Ages of Austerity

Warming-Up Activities

1. Brainstorming on the Topic

緊縮財政とは何だろう？　イギリスでは第二次世界大戦中・戦後によくこの言葉が使われたが、近年もまたこの言葉が使われるようになった。イギリスで、第二次世界大戦中・戦後にどんなことが起こったのだろう？（Chapter 1 参照）　また、21 世紀以降、どんなことが起こっているのだろう？

2. Vocabulary

- □ propaganda 名 プロパガンダ
- □ self-discipline 名 自制、自己鍛錬
- □ proliferate 自動 増殖する
- □ idealise, -ize 他動 〜を理想化する
- □ obscure 他動 〜を覆い隠す 形 不明瞭な
- □ comprehensive 形 包括的な
- □ deficit 名 不足分、赤字
- □ endorsement 名 是認、推奨（他動 endorse）
- □ sexism 名 性差別（> sexist 性差別主義者）
- □ condemn 自動 〜を非難する

🔊 **Audio 2-01**

'Keep Calm and Carry on.' Around 2008, this slogan, written in a sans-serif font with the Tudor Crown on top, suddenly began to make its way everywhere—from shopping bags to towels and mugs. You can easily find its parodies, too: 'Keep Calm and Have a Beer' and 'Now Panic and Freak Out', to name only two.

5 The slogan was originally in a propaganda poster designed by the government in 1939 in the feared event of a Nazi invasion. The government wanted the nation to maintain self-discipline with a 'stiff upper lip' as all British people are expected to do. The poster was never used because German troops never landed on Britain. It was first re-discovered in 2000, but the market had not proliferated until 2008, the

10 year of the global financial crisis and the UK government's first introduction of austerity measures—or when politicians started to say the country was entering a new 'age of austerity', the phrase formerly used for the wartime and post-war eras. Oddly enough, more than 10 million people watched *Call the Midwife* (2012–) in the 2010s as if to re-experience post-war austerity to make it easier to live in this

15 new age of austerity.

This is really an odd cultural phenomenon. In *The Ministry of Nostalgia* (2016), journalist Owen Hatherley calls it 'austerity nostalgia'. Austerity nostalgia not only idealises life in the age of austerity but also obscures the

20 obvious difference between the two ages of austerity. In the 1940s, the government struggled to create a Welfare State, construct a comprehensive system of education, and guarantee full employment. Now, Hatherley argues, the government is cutting public spendings to reduce the

The Ministry of Nostalgia
(Verso Books, 2016)

25 public deficit and increasing taxes to support the private sector. He mentions *Call the Midwife* as an endorsement of this 'right-wing phenomenon', but it may be a little misleading. This BBC series centres on midwives and nuns of an Anglican nursing convent in the poverty-stricken East End of London during the age of austerity. As Hatherley says, the series misrepresents working-class people as if

30 they all were and should be obedient. [A] However, it clearly defends the NHS, addresses the plight of the working class, and accuses bureaucracy, sexism and ableism. [B] Rather, the problem lies in its soft socialism. [C] It relies too much on

community spirit, goodwill and hard work on the part of common people. **[D]**

Can we just 'keep calm and carry on'? British film director Ken Loach believes we should not. He made two films about new challenges in this new age of 35

I, Daniel Blake (Entertainment One, 2016)

austerity: *I, Daniel Blake* (2016) and *Sorry We Missed You* (2019). *I, Daniel Blake* condemns cold-hearted bureaucracy, as endured by Daniel, an old widower, and 40 Katie, a young single mother. Although Daniel has had a heart attack and is prohibited by his doctor from working, he is considered fit by the government 45 and therefore unable to have a sick benefit. Katie cannot get help, either, because she arrives a little late for an appointment. Daniel wants to help her and her two little children, but he ends up applying for a job he cannot take in order to receive an unemployment benefit. *Sorry We Missed You* is even bleaker. Modestly hoping to lead a better life, Ricky decides to run a franchise as a 'self-employed' delivery 50 driver. Soon, he gets overwhelmed by pressure and exhausted by long-hour work resulting from a zero-hours contract. His family finally manage to recover mutual trust and decide to stick together. But the film does not end happily. Even though the rest of his family try to stop him, Ricky, now severely injured, drives off to work to pay the debts. That is, Loach warns us, what is happening and could 55 happen to anyone. No, we can't just 'keep calm and carry on'.

NOTES

l. 1: **sans-serif** 形 サンセリフの
l. 2: **Tudor Crown** チューダー朝の王冠 (イギリス王室のシンボル)
l. 4: **freak out** 自制心をなくして騒ぐ (俗)
l. 27: **Anglican** 形 イングランド国教会の、聖公会の
l. 28: **convent** 名 修道会、女子修道院
l. 31: **plight** 名 苦境、窮状
l. 32: **ableism** 名 障がい者差別
l. 40: **widower** 名 妻に先立たれた男性
l. 52: **zero-hours contract** ゼロ時間契約

1. The original purpose of the slogan 'Keep Calm and Carry On' was

   (A) to promote the sale of state-sponsored merchandise.

   (B) to encourage self-control during a potential invasion.

   (C) to express support for the government after the financial crisis.

   (D) to remember post-war austerity in a difficult time.

2. According to the passage, concrete examples of 'austerity nostalgia' include

   (A) consumer products with the slogan 'Keep Calm and Carry On'.

   (B) the government's effort to establish a better welfare system.

   (C) the expansion of the private sector in welfare and education.

   (D) the films like *I, Daniel Blake* and *Sorry We Missed You*.

3. [A], [B], [C] and [D] indicate where the following sentence can be added to paragraph 2. Mark your answer on your answer sheet.

   We all know that with these alone, people could not resolve all those problems.

4. Which of the following statements is true of *I, Daniel Blake* and *Sorry We Missed You*?

   (A) Both films underline the importance of self-discipline during hard times.

   (B) Neither of the two addresses the negative consequences of austerity measures.

   (C) *I, Daniel Blake* criticises the current welfare system for not functioning well.

   (D) *Sorry We Missed You* presents mutual trust as a solution to the current problems.

5.–7. Complete the summary below. Use one word only from the passage for each answer.

The passage explores the phenomenon of what Owen Hatherley calls 'austerity nostalgia' and contrasts it with the harsh realities of austerity. As in the sudden popularity of the slogan 'Keep Calm and Carry On', British people suddenly began to consume the age of austerity in the new age of austerity after the global financial crisis of 2008. This nostalgia at once makes it look easier to live in austerity and **5.**_____ the difference between post-war and current austerity. Through *I, Daniel Blake* and *Sorry We Missed You*, Ken Loach depicts the grim realities **6.**_____ by individuals. The passage concludes that 'Keep Calm and Carry On' is not an appropriate response to the new **7.**_____ of this new age of austerity.

Listening Comprehension ///

📶 **Audio 2-02**

Listen to part of a short presentation by Lily on a topic covered in the reading passage. Answer whether the following statements are **true** or **false**.

1. She reviews *I, Daniel Blake* favourably.   [   ]

2. The film is more than just a reminder of how powerless we are.   [   ]

3. The film inspires hope because both Daniel and Katie somehow get over the hardships.   [   ]

Both in Britain and in Japan, a style or fashion of the recent past steadily makes a comeback ('retro'). How do you compare 'austerity nostalgia' with retro? Or how do you compare 'austerity nostalgia' with Japanese cultural phenomena like 'Shōwa nostalgia' and 'Taishō roman'?

 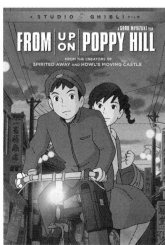

From Up On Poppy Hill
(STUDIO GHIBLI Inc., 2011)

Homework/Research ///

1. Watch *Sorry We Missed You* and then listen to Lily's presentation again. The recording ends before the end of her presentation. What do you think she wants to say in the final 30 seconds of her presentation? Or what would you say if you were Lily?

2. Read the passage again. Most problems covered in paragraph 3 can be found in Japan or in many developed countries. Find out more about one of those problems and make a policy proposal to resolve it.

Chapter 10
Climate Change: Policy, Opinion and Cultural Awareness

Warming-Up Activities

1. Brainstorming on the Topic

気候変動にどのくらい関心があるだろう？　気候変動についてどんなことを学んできただろう？　気候変動について一般市民はどんな行動を取っているだろう？　政府や企業に何をしてほしいと期待しているだろう？　以下のVocabularyから二つ以上の語を選んでブレインストーミングをし、ディスカッションしてみよう。

2. Vocabulary

☐ **target** 名 目標

☐ **carbon emission** （通例複数）二酸化炭素排出

☐ **subsidy** 名 補助金、助成金

☐ **fossil fuel** 化石燃料

☐ **optimistic** 形 楽観的な（対 pessimistic）

☐ **extreme weather** 異常気象、極端気象

☐ **climate fiction** 気候変動小説

☐ **mass extinction** 大量絶滅

☐ **renewable energy** 再生可能エネルギー

☐ **just transition** 公正な移行

🔊 Audio 2-03

Britain has failed to reach almost all of its targets for net zero carbon emissions, according to a 2023 report from the government's Climate Change Committee. In the same year, rumours circulated that the UK would break its promise to provide about 11 billion pounds of aid to countries suffering the effects of climate change. In 2019, the UK government was the first in the world to declare a climate emergency. Major achievements at the COP26 in Glasgow in 2021, including proposals to end subsidies to fossil fuels, were made thanks to the UK's influence. However, Britain has now lost its role as a global leader in the fight against climate change. Indeed, evidence suggests that the current Conservative government is charging in the opposite direction: In July of 2023, PM Rishi Sunak announced approval of more than one-hundred licences for oil and gas drilling in the North Sea.

These events come amidst growing concern among the British public about climate change. A 2021 survey found that 85% of Britons say they are concerned—almost half say 'very concerned'. The level of concern varies according to a number of factors, including political affiliation and gender: Labour supporters are significantly more concerned than Conservatives, and women are more anxious than men. Similarly, almost three-quarters think that the effects of climate change are now being felt, while about 20% think the effects will be seen in ten or more years. These data show a clear shift in public opinion over the past ten years. What is less clear is how much ordinary Britons are willing to change their lifestyles to help fight climate change. Only 30% think people are willing to stop eating meat; 37% think people will choose alternatives to driving; and only 22% think people will fly less often. People are, however, more optimistic about the switch to green technologies such as solar panels and electric cars.

Extreme weather events in the UK have surely helped shift opinion. The summer of 2022 was the hottest on record with temperatures reaching 40° C for the first time ever. Protests by major environmental groups such as Extinction Rebellion, Insulate Britain and Just Stop Oil have raised public awareness—often in shocking, controversial ways. Local protests are multiplying across Britain. During a span of just two weeks in 2021, some 280 local campaigns were added to the National Grassroots Campaign Map. However, media and politicians have tended to ignore or downplay the significance of these protests.

In *Climate Crisis and the 21st Century British Novel* (2017), Astrid Bracke argues that contemporary literature is an important part of our cultural 35 awareness of the crisis. Novels such as Ian McEwan's *Solar* (2010) and *Nutshell* (2016) show us the complex attitudes of individuals, including 'denial, scepticism and cognitive dissonance'. 40 Cognitive dissonance means living our daily lives as if nothing is wrong even though we know that our world is being destroyed. A new kind of writing called climate fiction, or 'cli fi', imagines the 45

Solar (Random House, 2010)

Nutshell (Jonathan Cape, 2016)

past, present or future effects of climate change on the planet. While there is a long British tradition of science fiction about climate disaster, numerous novels, films and television series have appeared since 2000. A television 'eco-thriller' called *The Rig* premiered just before PM Sunak announced expanded oil and gas drilling in the North Sea. The series follows the crew of an oil rig trapped in 50 a mysterious fog. As tremors strike the rig, ash rains down, infecting some of the crew. Company geologist Rose believes the drilling has awakened an ancient creature associated with mass extinctions in the past. As the crisis unfolds, crew members worry about the future of the oil industry and its impact on the environment. Rose thinks that instead of pursuing the last drop of oil, companies 55 can change to renewable energy while insuring a just transition to new jobs. Now, if only *this* bit of fiction could become reality.

NOTES

l. 1: **net zero** ネットゼロ、実質ゼロ（温室効果ガスの排出が吸収量と等しくなり、実質的な排出量がゼロになる状態のことを指し、イギリス政府の Net Zero Strategy は 2050 年までに実質排出量ゼロを目標としている <www.gov.uk/government/publications/net-zero-strategy>）

ll. 2-3: **Climate Change Committee** 気候変動委員会（2008 年の気候変動法に基づいて設立された独立した政府機関で、気候変動への対応や目標排出量についての提言や報告をおこなう）

l. 6: **COP26** 2021 年 11 月 13 日にスコットランドのグラスゴーで開催された国連の気候変動に関する会議（COP = Conference of Parties）

l. 33: **downplay** 他動 ～を重視しない、軽く扱う

l. 40: **dissonance** 名 不協和（cognitive dissonance の意味は本文参照）

l. 49: **rig** 名 リグ（油田の掘削装置）

l. 51: **tremor** 名 震え、震動

1. According to the author,
   (A) Britain is a global leader in the fight against climate change.
   (B) there is lack of concern about climate change among the British public.
   (C) there is widespread protest in the UK, including national and local campaigns.
   (D) British literature of the 21st century has failed to deal with the climate crisis.

2. The following facts from paragraph 2 are true EXCEPT:
   (A) A large majority of Britons are concerned about climate change.
   (B) Conservatives are more concerned than supporters of Labour.
   (C) People believe that green technologies hold promise for the future.
   (D) People are less optimistic about making changes in lifestyle.

3. According to paragraph 3, all of the following statements are true EXCEPT:
   (A) Politicians and media have paid little attention to the growing number of local protests.
   (B) Record-high temperatures and extreme weather have influenced public opinion.
   (C) Some environmental protests have stirred controversy.
   (D) Just Stop Oil organised more than 280 campaigns across Britain.

4. Cognitive dissonance around climate change means
   (A) changing one's lifestyle to help reduce its impact.
   (B) being sceptical about whether humans are really causing climate change.
   (C) ignoring the crisis.
   (D) knowing the crisis exists but continuing to live as if nothing is wrong.

5.–7. Complete the summary of paragraph 4 below. Choose one word only from the passage for each answer.

Contemporary ⁵·_____ is an important indicator of the cultural awareness of climate change. Climate fiction ⁶·_____ drastic changes to the planet through stories set in past, present or future. In the TV eco-thriller *The Rig*, an ⁷·_____ creature is awakened in the North Sea.

Listening Comprehension ///

🔊 Audio 2-04

Listen to the summary of findings from the UK 2023 Climate Change Committee report. Make notes and answer whether the following statements are **true** or **false**.

1. The report says that governments failed to act on many of its programmes and policies. [   ]

2. Programmes related to the energy efficiency and heating of UK homes have achieved strong results. [   ]

3. The government does not have a programme for educating the public about more eco-friendly lifestyle changes. [   ]

Discussion ////

1. Which kind of climate action do you think is most effective overall: high-profile campaigners and events organised by environmental groups or local campaigns organised by concerned citizens? Discuss the merits and demerits of each.

2. What lifestyle changes would you be willing to make to help in the fight against climate change?

3. Discuss the state of climate change awareness in Japan or in another country with which you are familiar.

Homework/Research ////

1. Choose a British climate novel or film and discuss character, setting and plot along with one or more of the issues that it raises.

2. Research Japan's efforts to reduce carbon emissions. How do Japan's efforts compare to those in the UK?

Chapter 11
Cotton Capital: Britain and the Slave Trade

Warming-Up Activities

1. Brainstorming on the Topic

アメリカ合衆国の奴隷制度について高校でどんなことを習っただろう？ イギリスがどのように奴隷制に関わったか知っているだろうか？ 学校で習った事柄を別の視点から見たものを学んだことがあるだろうか？

2. Vocabulary

☐ philanthropist 名 博愛主義者
☐ topple 自動 ばったり倒れる 他動 〜を倒す
☐ ledger 名 台帳
☐ archive 名 文書館、保管文書、アーカイブ
☐ enslave 他動 〜を奴隷にする

☐ unsavoury, -vory 名 不快な、道徳的に芳しくない
☐ captive 形 捕虜の、囚われた
☐ ongoing 形 継続中の
☐ abolition 名 廃止
☐ reimburse 他動 〜に費用を払い戻す、弁済する

The murder of George Floyd in the US in 2020 sparked a wave of Black Lives Matter (BLM) protests globally. One of the scenes of protest was Bristol, England, where a crowd pulled down a statue of Edward Colston, dragged and rolled it through town and dumped it in the harbour. Edward Colston was a successful
5 merchant, generous philanthropist and Member of Parliament. He also acquired his vast fortune through the slave trade as a senior executive in the Royal African Company.

For Katharine Viner, editor-in-chief of *The Guardian* newspaper, the BLM protests and the toppling of Colston's statue were a call for an awakening across
10 Britain and specifically a call for *The Guardian* (founded in 1821) to look deeply into its own past with possible connections to the cotton trade and slavery. To do so, *The Guardian* commissioned Cassandra Gooptar, a post-doctoral research fellow, to look for any hard evidence connecting the newspaper's past with slavery. After months of searching, Gooptar happened upon a commercial ledger from 1822 in
15 the archives of the Derbyshire Record Office containing the names of enslavers who ran cotton plantations in the United States along the Florida coast and the Sea Islands off Georgia and South Carolina. And on one page someone had written the name of a company buying cotton: Shuttleworth, Taylor & Co. The Taylor in the company was John Edward Taylor, the founder of *The Manchester Guardian* (now
20 *The Guardian*). In addition, nine out of eleven of Taylor's financial backers were also involved in the cotton trade (one co-owning a plantation). Here was proof that Taylor was involved in importing cotton picked by slaves and, thus, directly connecting *The Guardian* to the use of enslaved people on plantations in the United States.

Historian Nicholas Draper of University College London has suggested that
25 largely due to the global spread of the BLM movement Britons are only recently becoming aware of how many aristocrats became wealthy from slavery. And it is not only *The Guardian* that is having to reckon with its connection to the slave trade. Numerous other corporations, banks, universities, charities, even the Church of England are discovering that they, too, are having to deal with the same
30 unsavoury facts. Draper goes on to note that for many Britons the need to face history becomes doubly difficult because it flies in the face of the narrative they have been taught: 'Slavery was a terrible thing, but we were responsive to it, we did

away with it and we expunged that stain from the British nation.' This narrative, though, has no way to recognise the historical fact that the British slave trade to the Caribbean from West Africa began officially in 1663 with a royal charter 35 granted to the 'Company of Royal Adventurers of England Trading into Africa' (later shortened to the aforementioned 'Royal African Company') and by the mid-18th century, England was the biggest shipper of captive Africans in the world.

    The Guardian's response to the need to face history has been to create an ongoing multimedia special series based on Cassandra Gooptar's research: 40 *Cotton Capital: How Slavery Changed 'The Guardian', Britain and the World.* The project incorporates online essays, podcasts, video presentations, artwork and photography by Black artists, a newsletter and 'deep dives' into the history and lives of 45 enslaved people connected with *The Guardian*. The newspaper's editor-in-chief has stated that the goal of the series is to confront and apologise for *The Guardian*'s role 50 in the slave trade. And perhaps *Cotton Capital* may in some way contribute towards a new British national narrative.

How Slavery Changed 'The Guardian', Britain and the World (https://www.theguardian.com/news/series/cotton-capital)

NOTES

ll. 1-2: **Black Lives Matter** ブラック・ライヴズ・マター運動 (アメリカ合衆国のアフリカ系アメリカ人コミュニティから国際的に波及した、黒人に対する暴力の根絶や制度的人種差別の撤廃を求める運動)

l. 2: **Bristol** ブリストル (イングランド西部の都市)

ll. 6-7: **the Royal African Company** 王立アフリカ会社 (詳細は本文)

l. 12: **post-doctoral research fellow** 博士号研究員、ポスドク研究員

l. 15: **Derbyshire** ダービーシャー (イングランド北部の州)

ll. 16-17: **the Sea Islands** シー諸島 (アメリカ合衆国南部のジョージア州とサウスカロライナ州沖にある島々)

l. 24: **University College London** ロンドン大学ユニヴァーシティ・コレッジ (アメリカ英語の **college** と意味が違うので注意)

l. 37: **aforementioned** 形 上述の

1. We can infer from paragraph 1 that the crowd dumped the statue of Edward Colston in the harbour because

   (A) they were drunk.

   (B) they did not like the statue.

   (C) they disapproved of Edward Colston.

   (D) Edward Colston was richer than they were.

2. *The Guardian* hired Cassandra Gooptar to

   (A) work for Shuttleworth, Taylor & Co.

   (B) investigate *The Guardian*'s past and its founder.

   (C) clean and repair Edward Colston's statue.

   (D) steal the ledger from the Derbyshire Record Office archives.

3. According to paragraph 2, what did Cassandra Gooptar find in the ledger in the Derbyshire Record Office archives?

   (A) The name of the company in which Taylor was a partner.

   (B) The name of Taylor's bank and his account number.

   (C) A photograph of Taylor visiting a plantation in the United States.

   (D) Some samples of cotton picked by enslaved people.

4. According to paragraph 4, what is NOT true about *Cotton Capital*?

   (A) It is a multimedia project.

   (B) It has already changed the world.

   (C) It is based on Cassandra Gooptar's research.

   (D) It is an ongoing project.

5.–7. Complete the summary below. Choose one word only from the passage for each answer.

According to historian Nicholas Draper, Britons are only **5.**_____ becoming aware of how much money was coming into Britain because of slavery. Furthermore, it is difficult for Britons to face the facts of Britain's involvement in the slave trade because it is not the **6.**_____ they were taught. For example, it is hard to fathom that Britain was at one time the **7.**_____ shipper of enslaved people around the world.

Listening Comprehension ///

 Audio 2-06

Listen to the conversation between two students. Answer whether the following statements are **true** or **false**.

1. After 1833, Britain continued to be involved in the buying and selling of slaves but not the buying and selling of cotton. [　　]

2. According to Miho, the history of Britain's involvement in the slave trade is a very complicated story. [　　]

3. Miho's explanation is helpful but Nick feels he needs to learn more. [　　]

Discussion

What do you think about *Cotton Capital, The Guardian*'s extensive, in-depth multimedia production about Britain and the slave trade? Some people see this as a sincere and useful effort. However, some readers have accused *The Guardian* of 'virtue signalling', feeling they were just making a public demonstration of taking a moral stance. Others feel that even if it's just an apology for the past, it's a necessary first step. What do you think?

Homework/Research

1. Watch *The Guardian*'s initial panel discussion about *Cotton Capital: The Guardian's Founders and Transatlantic Slavery*.

www.youtube.com/watch?v=G_d3DCNEt6M

2. Go to the *Cotton Capital* website and browse around in it. How do you feel about the multimedia format? Which parts did you find most interesting or useful? Essays? Videos? Podcasts? Share your experience with other students.

http://www.theguardian.com/news/series/cotton-capital

Chapter 12
A Hostile Environment: The Windrush Scandal

Warming-Up Activities

1. Brainstorming on the Topic

かつてのイギリス植民地であった国のうち、どんな国のことを知っているだろう？ 大英帝国（the British Empire）、イギリス連合王国（the United Kingdom）、イギリス連邦（the British Commonwealth）の違いを正確に言えるだろうか。

2. Vocabulary

☐ **recruit** 他動 ～を入れる、補充する

☐ **emigrate** 自動 移住する、移出する

☐ **restrict** 他動 ～を制限する

☐ **threaten** 他動 ～を脅す、威嚇する

☐ **deportation** 名 国外追放、強制送還

☐ **detention** 名 拘留

☐ **hostile** 形 敵意がある、敵対的な

☐ **descendant** 名 子孫

☐ **reversal** 名 逆転

☐ **proclaim** 他動 ～を宣言する、高らかに言う

With the end of the Second World War, Britain was faced with years of rebuilding. The war left England with a broken economy and more than two million homes destroyed or badly damaged along with roads, bridges, factories and transportation links in ruins. To fill the need for thousands of workers, the British
5 government actively recruited workers from British colonies in the Caribbean with the opportunity of living and working in England. According to the British Nationality Act of 1948, citizens of British colonies were automatically British subjects with the right to live and work in the United Kingdom permanently. As a result, between 1948 and 1973 half a million people emigrated primarily from
10 Jamaica, but also from other islands such as Trinidad, Barbados, Grenada and St Lucia. These immigrants became known as the 'Windrush generation'—after the 'Empire Windrush', one of the first ships to bring the new Caribbean residents to Britain.

However, with a growing public concern about perceived uncontrolled
15 large-scale immigration from Commonwealth countries, the Conservative government passed the 1971 Immigration Act, which severely restricted the possibility of permanent residency as British subjects for immigrants arriving prior to 1973 (essentially the majority of the Windrush generation). As a result, many Caribbean immigrants found that they were no longer still British subjects as they
20 had believed. In addition, their children discovered, much to their surprise, that they had 'immigrant status' rather than permanent residency or even citizenship in a country where they had been born and raised. And when these 'citizens of nowhere' challenged their status as immigrants, they were often threatened with deportation.

25 Immigrants who had been recruited and encouraged by the British government to come and work in Britain now found themselves residing as undocumented immigrants. The right to remain in the UK as legal residents depended on individuals being able to prove residency predating 1973 by producing official documentation for each year. Unfortunately, this was often an
30 impossible burden considering that the Home Office had destroyed thousands of landing cards and other records of the original Windrush immigrants. People who had done nothing wrong now found themselves in danger of losing access to

necessities such as housing, health care, bank accounts, and driving licences, as well as being threatened with detention and deportation.

The crisis came to a head in 2012 when, under pressure to 'look tough on immigration', the Conservative government under David Cameron began requiring evidence of legal immigration for acquiring employment, housing and health care. As Theresa May, the then Home Secretary, stated: 'the aim is to create here in Britain a really hostile environment for illegal immigration.' The goal was to make the UK unliveable for undocumented immigrants and encourage 'self-deportation'. The result, though, was that members of the Windrush generation and their descendants were now also technically illegal immigrants.

However, in 2017, Amelia Gentleman, a reporter for *The Guardian* newspaper, investigated and reported on the ongoing Windrush scandal. She brought to the public's attention the hundreds of Commonwealth citizens, including the Windrush generation, who had been wrongly deported and denied their legal rights as British subjects. In April 2018, the Home Secretary, Sajid Javid, announced a reversal of the 'hostile environment' immigration policy, commissioned a 'Windrush Lessons Learned Review' and introduced a plan by which these British subjects could now apply for British passports. Twenty-four hours after the announcement, the British television programme *Channel 4 News* hosted a live-streamed debate on the Windrush scandal involving members of the Windrush generation, their children, British politicians and other public figures. In 2023, on the 75th anniversary of the arrival of the 'Empire Windrush', the British government officially proclaimed 22 June as 'Windrush Day'. The question remains, though, what is being celebrated and by whom?

NOTES

ll. 6-7: **the British Nationality Act** イギリス国籍法

ll. 10-11: **Trinidad, Barbados, Grenada and St Lucia** トリニダード、バルバドス、グレナダ、セント・ルシア（すべてカリブ海の国々）

l. 30: **Home Office** 内務省

l. 38: **Home Secretary** 内務大臣

1. According to the British Nationality Act of 1948, citizens of British colonies
   (A) could apply for British citizenship and live and work in the UK.
   (B) were also considered to be British subjects and allowed to live and work in the UK.
   (C) had to give up their colonial citizenship and become British citizens in order to be able to live and work in the UK.
   (D) were automatically registered as undocumented immigrants once they entered the UK.

2. In paragraph 2, the author implies that many British citizens were concerned that
   (A) there were no longer enough workers coming to Britain due to restricted immigration.
   (B) they were becoming 'citizens of nowhere' due to the declining economy.
   (C) there were too many 'non-British' people coming to live and work in the UK.
   (D) the majority of the Windrush generation were being treated unfairly by the British government.

3. According to paragraph 3, it was difficult for members of the Windrush generation to prove their status as legal residents in the UK because
   (A) they could not read and write English well.
   (B) they could not afford to pay for the necessary documents.
   (C) the government threatened to detain or deport them if they tried.
   (D) the government had destroyed many of the necessary documents.

4. Amelia Gentleman's investigation showed that
   (A) many Commonwealth citizens had been denied their legal rights.
   (B) *The Guardian* newspaper had created the 'hostile environment'.
   (C) the 'Empire Windrush' had arrived in Britain on 22 June 1948.
   (D) the British government had 'learned a lesson'.

5.–7. Complete the summary below. Choose one word only from the passage for each answer.

According to the British Nationality Act of 1948, colonial citizens were now also British subjects. However, the 1971 Immigration Act **5.**_____ the possibility for immigrants to become **6.**_____ residents of the UK. In 2012, the Home Office stated that its goal was to make the UK **7.**_____ for illegal immigrants. However, Amelia Gentleman, in 2017, reported that hundreds of Commonwealth immigrants to the UK had been denied their legal rights.

Listening Comprehension ////

🔊 Audio 2-08

Listen to the conversation between Max and Maggie about a video they are watching. Answer whether the following statements are **true** or **false**.

1. Max is not aware of what the Windrush Scandal is.   [   ]

2. Helen Joseph was one of the people featured on the   [   ]
   'Windrush Scandal' debate.

3. 'Citizens of nowhere' refers to British citizens who   [   ]
   emigrated from the West Indies.

Discussion

1. Based on the reading passage and the dialogue, what do you think 'citizens of nowhere' means? What do you think should be required to get a passport? What are the requirements for a Japanese passport?

2. 22 June is now officially National Windrush Day in the United Kingdom. If you were a member of the Windrush generation or one of their descendants, what do you think your feelings would be about this?

Homework/Research

1. Watch the 'Windrush Scandal' video:

   www.channel4.com/news/the-windrush-generation-fighting-to-be-british

   What different points of view do you hear? Which do you agree or disagree with?

2. If your school library has a copy of Amelia Gentleman's *The Windrush Betrayal: Exposing the Hostile Environment*, read the 'Introduction' and be ready to discuss.

Chapter 13
Behind the Glamour of 'Dishi Rishi'

Warming-Up Activities

1. Brainstorming on the Topic

イギリスのスナク首相についてどんなことを知っているだろう？　また、イギリスにおけるアジア系住民にはどのような地域の出身者が多いのだろう？　どのような文化や信仰を持つ人がいて、どのような問題に直面しているのだろう？

2. Vocabulary

□ oppression 名 圧政、抑圧

□ racism 名 人種差別（> racist 人種差別主義者）

□ census 名 国勢調査

□ vicious 形 悪性の

□ descent 名 家系、出自、降下

□ aggravate 他動 〜を悪化させる

□ designate 他動 〜を明示する、指定する

□ discriminate 自動 差別する（名 discrimination）

□ intensify 他動 〜を強化する

□ toxic 形 有毒な、害悪をもたらす

On 25 October 2022, Rishi Sunak, a Conservative MP, became the first British Indian and Hindu to hold the office of prime minister. Nicknamed 'Dishi Rishi', this good-looking man in fashionable suits has everything: privileged education, wealth and power. He was admitted to Winchester College, one of 5 the best public schools in England. After graduating from Winchester and the University of Oxford, he went on to study for an MBA in the US, where he met his future wife, Akshata Murty, the only daughter of an Indian business billionaire. Now, he is richer than King Charles III. When Liz Truss resigned as Prime Minister and Leader of the Conservative Party, she did not dissolve parliament and there 10 was no general election. All you had to do to reach 10 Downing Street was win the Conservative Party leadership election. Only Sunak and Penny Mordaunt entered, but Mordant pulled out of the race. Sunak just ran solo to the finish line.

Sunak is not the first successful British Asian in politics. Even in the Victorian era, a couple of Indians were elected to the House of Commons. 15 After the end of the British colonial rule, the Indian subcontinent was divided into Hindu-majority India and Muslim-majority Pakistan (the eastern region of which became Bangladesh in 1971). They came into conflict with each other. Many people migrated to Britain to escape political turmoil and seek better job opportunities. Some pursued a career in the arts and entertainment industry. In 20 the 1970s, Freddie Mercury, a British Indian, achieved international fame as the lead vocalist of the rock band Queen. But it was not until the 21st century that their presence had been highly visible in British politics. In 2016, Sadiq Khan, a Labour politician, became the first British Pakistani and Muslim to serve as Mayor of London. In 2019, Apsana Begum, a British Bangladeshi, became the 25 UK's first hijab-wearing MP. The hijab is more like a political statement now. While some regard it as an endorsement of oppression of Muslim women in Islam, others criticise such a view as an example of cultural imperialism.

However, these success stories obscure the grim realities. Needless to say, not all British Asians live happily or comfortably. According to the survey done by 30 a think-tank, 80% of British Indians have faced racism. The situation is worse for British Muslims—mostly Pakistani and Bangladeshi—who make up 6.5% of the population, according to the 2021 UK Census. The statistics show that 39% live in the most deprived areas of England and Wales, and 61% in relatively deprived areas. Unable to get out of the cycles of poverty, younger generations often feel frustrated. There is another vicious circle: hate and violence. While an international 'Islamist' 35 terrorist organisation was responsible for the 9/11 terrorist attacks in the US in 2001, the 7/7 bombings in London in 2005 were perpetrated by four 'homegrown' attackers, three of whom were young, British-born, radicalised Muslims of Pakistani descent. Many British people were worried that there was something wrong with Muslims. Some went so far as to abuse or express Islamophobia, or 40 hatred towards Muslims. The government's counter-terrorism strategy called 'Prevent' is supposed to prevent citizens from being radicalised, but scholars criticise it for aggravating the tension. It disproportionately designates Muslim-majority districts as 'priority areas' as if all Muslims were potential terrorists. After the 2011 revision, the government can even blacklist anyone for 'vocal and active 45 opposition to British values'. 'Where is our freedom of thought?' critics wonder. They argue Prevent has made this abnormal condition look normal and made it seem acceptable to discriminate against Muslims. As most social media platforms are programmed to remove hateful posts, we rarely come across extremely racist language. Even so, people do express hate and Islamophobia under the pretence of 50 condemning terrorism. Constantly exposed to hate and micro-aggressions, some extremely frustrated Muslims become <u>prone</u> to anger or, worse, violence. Their reckless behaviour, in turn, intensifies fear and hate. We really need to end this toxic loop.

NOTES

l. 4: **Winchester College** ウィンチェスター校 (ここでの college は中等学校の意)
l. 5: **public schools > public school** パブリックスクール (名門私立学校)
l. 6: **MBA** 経営学修士 (= **Master of Business Administration**)
l. 9: **dissolve parliament** 国会を解散する
l. 10: **10 Downing Street** ダウニング街 10 番地 (転じて内閣総理大臣官邸)
l. 14: **the House of Commons** 下院、庶民院 (イギリスの国会は二院制)
l. 15: **the Indian subcontinent** インド亜大陸
l. 18: **turmoil** 名 大混乱、混迷
l. 25: **hijab** 名 ヒジャブ
l. 35: **Islamist** 形 イスラーム主義の (イスラームの教えに基づく政治を実現しようとする運動)
l. 37: **perpetrated > perpetrate** 他動 ～ (悪事など) を犯す、おこなう
l. 38: **radicalised > radicalise, -ize** 他動 ～を過激化させる
l. 43: **disproportionately** 副 不釣り合いに

1. According to paragraph 1, Rishi Sunak

    (A) is the first British Asian member of the UK Parliament.

    (B) can be described as a man of modest education.

    (C) became a billionaire due to his hard work.

    (D) became Leader of the Conservative Party without a ballot.

2. Which of the following statements is true of British Asians?

    (A) They were barred from politics in the Victorian era.

    (B) Their success in music predated their success in politics.

    (C) Sadiq Khan was the first British Pakistani to fill a key cabinet post.

    (D) Apsana Begum is not only a politician but also a fashion influencer.

3. The word prone in paragraph 3 is closest in meaning to

    (A) inclined.

    (B) inevitable.

    (C) inherent.

    (D) internal.

4. In paragraph 3, the author suggests that British people should

    (A) sacrifice their freedom for the sake of national security.

    (B) put social media under the state's control to stop terrorism.

    (C) understand the role of social media in the counter-terrorism strategy.

    (D) break the harmful chain reaction of hate and violence.

5.–7. Complete the notes below. Use one word only from the passage for each answer.

- Many South Asians emigrated to Britain in order to ^{5.}_____ conflicts after the withdrawal of the British.
- A large number of British Muslims live in districts where many residents suffer from ^{6.}_____.
- It is impossible to post hateful remarks on social media because most platforms have some algorithm to ^{7.}_____ them.

Listening Comprehension ////

🔊 Audio 2-10

Listen to the conversation between two students, Seojun and Mina, about the reading passage. Answer whether the following statements are **true** or **false**.

1. Mina often talks about anti-Asian racism and Islamophobia with her family members. [   ]

2. Thanks to the popularity of Black music, Americans no longer discriminate against Black people. [   ]

3. The success of K-Pop did not eradicate hate against or increase the visibility of Korean Japanese. [   ]

Discussion ///

1. There are quite a few politicians, journalists, musicians, actors and athletes of South Asian descent in Britain. Why do you think the Japanese media rarely tells us about them?

2. Listen to the dialogue again. Seojun and Mina compare the problems discussed in the reading passage with the problems in the US and Japan. How similar or how different are those problems? Use specific examples and reasons to support your opinion.

Homework/Research ///

The recording ends before the end of this conversation. What do you think Mina wanted to say? Watch films and/or television series like *Brick Lane* (2007) and the BBC's *Bodyguard* (2018–), and see how they represent Muslim women. Alternatively, read books and articles or watch documentaries on this subject. Then, write down what you would say if you were Mina.

Chapter **14**
J. K. Rowling and Transgender

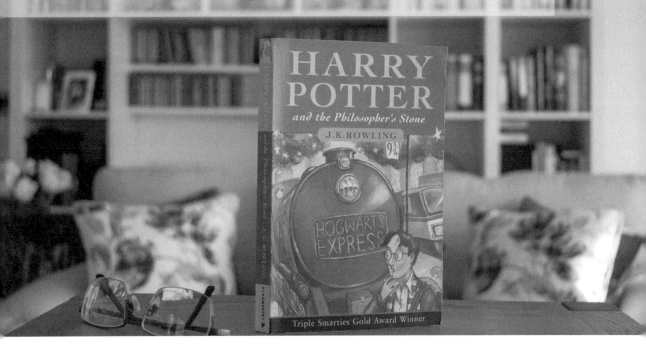

Warming-Up Activities

1. Brainstorming on the Topic

『ハリー・ポッター』の著者 J. K. Rowling について知っていることを書き出してみよう。彼女はどのような考え方の持ち主だろう？　また、「トランスジェンダー」や「トランスフォビア」について知っていることを書き出してみよう。

2. Vocabulary

☐ **transgender** 名 トランスジェンダー

☐ **cisgender** 名 シスジェンダー

☐ **identify** 他動 〜を (**as ...** として) 認める

☐ **spectrum** 名 スペクトル、範囲、連続体

☐ **offensive** 形 侮辱的 (攻撃的) な (他動 **offend**)

☐ **dignity** 名 尊厳

☐ **solidarity** 名 連帯

☐ **predatory** 形 捕食性の、人を食い物にする

☐ **legitimate** 形 正当な、合法的な

☐ **exclusionary** 名 排他的な (対 **inclusive**)

Audio 2-11

On 19 December 2019, J. K. Rowling, the author of *Harry Potter*, upset the world by tweeting her support for Maya Forstater, a cisgender female researcher who failed to renew her contract with
5 a think-tank because of her hostile tweets on transgender people. Transgender, as opposed to cisgender, is a gender identity or expression that does not correspond to the biological sex one is given at birth. When the government was planning to allow
10 transgender people to identify themselves as their chosen gender, Forstater claimed that M-to-F (male-

J. K. Rowling

to-female) transgender cannot and must not be regarded as women. Rowling supported her by using vulgar expressions. She constantly criticised sexism from a feminist perspective. Naturally, many transgender fans of *Harry Potter* showed
15 their disappointment.

Rowling did not stop there. On 6 June 2020, she tweeted again: '"People who menstruate". I'm sure there used to be a word for those people. Someone help me out. Wumben? Wimpund? Woomud?' It was not funny at all. Not only transgender people but also people across gender, sexuality and the whole
20 spectrum of difference found it offensive and began to suspect she may well be called 'transphobic'. Two days later, Daniel Radcliffe, who played Harry Potter in the film franchise, spoke out against the author: 'Transgender women are women. Any statement to the contrary erases the identity and dignity of transgender people and goes against all advice given by professional health care associations who have
25 far more expertise on this subject matter than either Jo or I.' Another two days later, Rowling defended herself. On the same day, Emma Watson, who portrayed Hermione, expressed her solidarity with transgender people. The controversy escalated. In February 2023, Rowling defended herself again in a podcast entitled *The Witch Trials of J. K. Rowling*.

30 We often assume that feminists are supportive of gender and sexual minorities, but why can self-proclaimed feminists like Rowling be so hostile to transgender people and activists? She always argues that all cisgender women

must not have their gender hijacked by those not born with uteri, and she often described transgender people as predatory men who just want to sneak into women-only spaces (e.g. public toilets) by posing as transgender. It all sounds 35 as if it were morally acceptable to discriminate against M-to-F transgender and treat them like criminals to protect cisgender women. There are radical feminists who embrace Rowling's view. While many feminists find it better to include transgender women, some radical feminists claim that they should keep them out of women-only spaces and organisations. Those feminists are called 'TERF' 40 (transgender-exclusionary radical feminists) as opposed to 'transgender-inclusive' feminists. TERF was, and still is, a legitimate analytical term used by scholars, but it has been used as an abuse. Indeed, many angry people called Rowling a TERF on social media as if the term were a byword for 'sexist'. Those transgender-exclusionary feminists began to call themselves 'gender-critical'. The tension 45 between transgender-inclusive and transgender-exclusionary feminists is said to be particularly high in the UK. Some call it a 'TERF war'.

　　While many British people think transphobia is a problem, they do not agree on how to tackle it. According to a market research company's 2020 survey, a large majority (70%) of British people over 18 across generations think that transgender 50 people are still facing discrimination, but 56% of Generation Z (born between 1996 and 2002) supported a further move to ensure transgender rights, while only 20% of baby boomers (born between 1945 and 1965) did. According to the 2020 government survey, 50% of British people supported transgender people's right to self-identify, while only 27% were against self-identification. The figures were 55 higher for women (57%), Londoners (59%) and supporters of Labour Party (70%), but they were lower for the rest. Unfortunately, there is no magic to fill these gaps.

l. 2: **tweeting > tweet** 他動 〜をツイートする (2023 年 7 月に X に改称した SNS への投稿) 名 ツイート
l. 17: **menstruate** 自動 生理がある
l. 22: **franchise** 名 フランチャイズ、シリーズ
l. 26: **portrayed > portray** 他動 〜を演じる
l. 28: **podcast** 名 ポッドキャスト
l. 33: **uteri > uterus** 名 子宮
l. 44: **byword** 名 典型、異名

1. Many transgender fans of *Harry Potter* were disappointed at J. K. Rowling's tweet mainly because of

   (A) her passionate support for a cisgender person.

   (B) her denial of transgender self-identification.

   (C) her constant promotion of feminist perspectives.

   (D) her frequent use of offensive language.

2. According to paragraph 2, Daniel Radcliffe

   (A) spoke against J. K. Rowling and came out as transgender himself.

   (B) suggested that J. K. Rowling's tweet was an insult to transgender people.

   (C) criticised J. K. Rowling's comment on transgender for its vulgar language.

   (D) ordered J. K. Rowling to respect the dignity of transgender people.

3. It can be inferred from paragraph 3 that the conflict between 'transgender-inclusive' and 'transgender-exclusionary' feminists in the UK primarily revolves around

   (A) J. K. Rowling's personality.

   (B) discrimination faced by transgender individuals.

   (C) varying opinions on self-identification.

   (D) the role of gender in society.

4. According to paragraph 4, British people are divided on transgender issues across all the lines EXCEPT

   (A) political views.

   (B) generation.

   (C) region.

   (D) race.

5.–7. Do the following statements agree with the information given in the passage? Write **true** (the statement agrees with the information), **false** (the statement contradicts the information) or **not given** (there is no information on this).

5. Transgender people include gay men who identify as male.

6. According to transgender-exclusionary radical feminists, sex is biologically determined and therefore none of those born as male has the right to self-identify with a woman.

7. Country dwellers and Conservative supporters are more likely to be transgender-exclusionary feminists.

Listening Comprehension ///

 Audio 2-12

Listen to the conversation between two students, Sophie and Rena, about the reading passage. Complete the following notes. Use one word only from the dialogue for each answer.

• While Rena was shocked at Rowling's comments, Sophie already knew the ¹._____ they provoked.

• Both Rena and Sophie think that Rowling is rather ²._____ because not all women menstruate, regardless of their sex by birth or gender identity.

• Rena thinks transgender people are not very ³._____ in Japan.

Discussion ////

1. Rowling's view of transgender affected and/or should affect your understanding of *Harry Potter* and *Fantastic Beasts*. Do you agree or disagree? If you are not familiar with *Harry Potter*, discuss whether the author's (or the filmmakers') political views affect your understanding of his/her/their novel or film.

2. Listen to the dialogue again. The recording ends when Rena begins to talk about her own generation. What do you think she wanted to say? What would you say if you were Rena?

Homework/Research ////

1. Watch films and television series like Tom Hooper's *The Danish Girl* (2015), Channel 4's *My Transsexual Summer* (2011) and the BBC's *Boy Meets Girl* (2015–16). Make a poster or a short video about their representation of transgender people.

2. Conduct a structured or semi-structured interview with three people of different social groups (e.g. age, gender, profession, nationality) about transgender rights. Make sure to get their consent and respect their privacy. Create a poster summing up your reseach.

Chapter 15
Gender in the UK: LGBTQ+ Issues

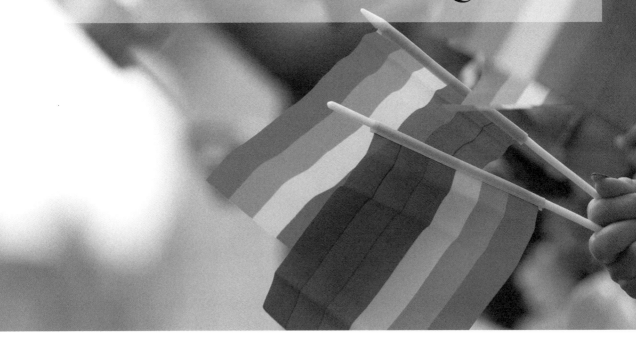

Warming-Up Activities

1. Brainstorming on the Topic

ゲイの権利や同性婚のようなジェンダーにまつわる問題のうち、何を知っているだろう？　ジェンダーとセクシュアリティーの違いを説明できるだろうか？　日本において、LGBTQ+ と呼ばれる人たちはどのような困難に直面しているだろう？

2. Vocabulary

☐ **gender dysphoria** ジェンダー・ディスフォリア（性別違和）
☐ **sexual orientation**　性的指向
☐ **gender reassignment**　性別再割当
☐ **decriminalise, -ize** 他動 ～を合法化する
☐ **recipient** 名 受取人、手術を受ける人

☐ **gender-affirming surgery**　性別適合手術
☐ **applaud** 他動 ～を賞賛する
☐ **epidemic** 名 流行病、突発的流行
☐ **diversify** 他動 ～を多様化する
☐ **graphic novel** （英米の）漫画（cf. manga）

The Marriage (Same Sex Couples) Act became law in England and Wales in July 2013. By mid-March 2014, couples were allowed to register their intent to marry, and shortly after the stroke of midnight on 29 March, the first same-sex couples in the United Kingdom exchanged marriage vows. Marriage not being a
5 requirement for adoption, same-sex adoption in the UK had become legal earlier: 2002 in England and Wales, 2009 in Scotland, and 2013 in Northern Ireland. And the legal status of transgender people began to be recognised. The Gender Recognition Act was passed in 2004, allowing people with gender dysphoria to change their legal gender and apply for a Gender Recognition Certificate. The
10 2010 Equality Act guarantees protection from discrimination or harassment for a number of characteristics, including sexual orientation and gender reassignment.

However, barely over fifty years ago homosexuality was still a criminal offence punishable by imprisonment. It was not until 1967 that homosexuality was decriminalised in the United Kingdom under the Sexual Offences Act. As might
15 be expected, 1967 also marked the beginning of an outpouring of British films pushing the boundaries of movie content by dealing more directly with LGBTQ+ (lesbian, gay, bisexual, transgendered, queer/questioning and others) issues. In response to this growing body of LGBTQ-themed films, the British Film Institute launched its London Lesbian and Gay Film Festival (LLGFF) in 1986 (now the
20 more inclusively titled BFI Flare: London LGBTQIA+ Film Festival).

The past half century has seen the release of such films as *Sunday Bloody Sunday* (1971) with its love triangle plot involving a bisexual man and his male and female lovers; *My Beautiful Laundrette* (1985), a Thatcher-era inter-racial, gay romance; Sally
25 Potter's *Orlando* (1992) starring Tilda Swinton as the time-travelling, sex-changing Orlando; *Lilting* (2014), a film combining gender issues with those of
30 ethnicity and culture; and *The Danish Girl* (2015) starring Eddie

The Danish Girl (Universal Pictures, 2016)

Redmayne, based loosely on the life of Lili Elbe, which tells the story of one of the first recipients of gender-affirming surgery. Though the film was applauded for its presentation of transgender issues, it also received criticism for having a cisgender 35 straight actor in the role of a transgender woman. Redmayne himself later said that he was not right for the part.

As with the film industry, television also began to open up to greater representation of LGBTQ+ characters and actors. The 1999 television programme, *Queer as Folk*, focused on the lives of three gay men living in Manchester. 40 Although generally well-received, it was noted that all three main characters were played by straight actors. The show was also criticised by some members of the gay community for not dealing at the time with more serious issues such as the AIDS epidemic. If *Queer as Folk* was a pioneering effort towards more diversified

Queer as Folk (Showtime, 2000-2005)

programming, the current Netflix series, *Heartstopper*, is the resulting progress. *Heartstopper* is essentially a teenage coming-of-age story with an extremely diversified LGBTQ+ cast. Created by British author Alice Oseman, the characters and storylines began as webcomics and graphic novels (with an online fanbase of 52+ million). The main characters are students at either Truham Grammar 45 School for Boys or Higgs Girls School, conveniently located close to each other. The series is noted for its positive representation of LGBTQ+ characters and for being strict about matching the sexual and racial identity of the actors with that of their characters. Series 1 and 2 are currently streaming with Series 3 scheduled for a 2024 release. 50

NOTES

l. 18: **the British Film Institute** 英国映画協会
ll. 45-46: **grammar school** グラマースクール (現在では、公立学校のうち選抜制の進学校を指す)

1. According to paragraph 1, which of the following statements is true regarding the Marriage (Same Sex Couples) Act?

    (A) Initially, it applied to only England.

    (B) It decriminalised homosexuality.

    (C) It allowed same-sex couples to marry.

    (D) It has been the law for over fifty years.

2. What is implied in paragraph 2 regarding the 1967 Sexual Offences Act?

    (A) It encouraged the making of LGBTQ-themed movies.

    (B) It discouraged the making of LGBTQ-themed movies.

    (C) It had no effect on the making of LGBTQ-themed movies.

    (D) It was passed due to the influence of LGBTQ-themed movies.

3. The author cites the films *My Beautiful Laundrette* and *Lilting* as examples of

    (A) films that focus on gay romance.

    (B) films made before homosexuality was decriminalised.

    (C) films that combine gender and cultural issues.

    (D) films promoted by the British Film Institute.

4. Which of the following statements is NOT true of *Queer as Folks*?

    (A) It focused on the lives of three gay men in Manchester.

    (B) The main characters were played by gay actors.

    (C) Some felt that the show did not deal with serious issues.

    (D) It helped move TV programming towards more diversification.

5. Complete the summary below. Choose one word only from the passage for each answer.

Heartstopper is a coming-of-age story with a very ^{5.}_____ cast. The story was ^{6.}_____ by Alice Oseman, who began by writing webcomics and graphic novels. The series is ^{7.}_____ for representing LGBTQ+ characters positively.

Listening Comprehension ///

🔊 Audio 2-14

Listen to the conversation between Haruka and Emma about the reading passage. Answer whether the following statements are **true** or **false**.

1. Haruka recommends that she and Emma watch   [   ]
   Heartstopper.

2. The sexual and racial identities of the actors in *Heartstopper*   [   ]
   match with the characters they play.

3. The more Emma watches *Heartstopper*, the more she likes it.   [   ]

What are some issues regarding gender and LGBTQ+ rights in Japan? After reading the passage, how do you think Japan compares with Britain on these issues? Give examples to support your view.

Homework/Research ////

1. Watch a few episodes of *Heartstopper* and be prepared to discuss in class.

2. Watch one of the films mentioned in the passage and prepare a short oral presentation about it. For a larger selection of LGBTQ-themed films, go to the British Film Institute's homepage: www.bfi.org.uk

The British Film Institute

人名・作品名など
※ リスニングに含まれているものを含む。なお、以下は本文登場順である。

Chapter 1

David Cameron デイヴィッド・キャメロン（1966
〜）。イギリスの政治家。元保守党党首、元首相。
本文で書かれている一件で知られる。

Arnold [J.] Toynbee アーノルド・J・トインビー
（1889 〜 1975）。イギリスの歴史家。全 12 巻
に及ぶ『歴史の研究』（*A Study of History*, 1934
〜 61）で有名。1960 年代までは広く読まれた。

Fintan O'Toole フィンタン・オトゥール（1958
〜）。アイルランドの文芸編集者、ジャーナリスト。
アイルランドのリベラル系高級紙『アイリッシュ・
タイムズ』（*The Irish Times*）のコラムニストとし
て有名。

Peter Shore ピーター・ショア（1924 〜 2001）。
イギリスの政治家。労働党議員。ハロルド・ウィ
ルソン（Harold Wilson, 1916 〜 95）政権下で経
済担当大臣や通商担当大臣などを歴任。ヨーロッ
パ経済共同体（EEC）加盟をめぐる議決で造反し
たことでも知られる。

(Adolf) Hitler アドルフ・ヒトラー（1889 〜 1945）。
ドイツの政治家。国家社会主義ドイツ労働者党
（ナチス）を率い、総統となって独裁体制を敷い
た。拡大主義的な外交政策は第二次世界大戦の引
き金となり、極端な人種主義はユダヤ人や障がい
者の迫害や虐殺にもつながった。

Roger Helmer ロジャー・ヘルマー（1944 〜）。
イギリスのビジネスマン。大手多国籍企業の
GM などを歴任した後、欧州議会議員へ転身。
保守党からイギリス独立党（UK Independence
Party = UKIP）へ鞍替え。ジェンダーや環境問題
に関する失言、公的資金の流用疑惑の渦中で体
調不良を理由に政界を引退。

Len Deighton レン・デイトン（1929 〜）。イギ
リスの作家。労働者階級出身の諜報員を主人公
としたスパイ小説で知られ、『イプクレス・ファ
イル』（*The Ipcress File*, 1962）や『ベルリンの
葬送』（*Funeral in Berlin*, 1964）などは映画化さ
れている（映画の邦題はそれぞれ『国際謀報局』と
『パーマーの危機脱出』）。代表作は、本文で触れ
られている『SS-GB』（*SS-GB*, 1978）。

SS-GB 『SS-GB』（1978）。レン・デイトンによる
歴史改変小説。2017 年に BBC で全 5 話ドラマ
化されている（邦題は『SS-GB ──ナチスが戦争
に勝利した世界』）。邦訳はハヤカワ文庫から出

版されている。

Robert Harris ロバート・ハリス（1957 〜）。イギ
リスの作家。ジャーナリストとして BBC やリ
ベラル系高級紙『ガーディアン』（*The Guardian*）
の政治部編集員を務めた後、『ファーザーランド』
（*Fatherland*, 1992）で小説家デビュー。

Fatherland 『ファーザーランド』（1992）。ロバー
ト・ハリスによる歴史改変小説。アメリカの
HBO で 1994 年にテレビ映画化されている。邦
訳は文春文庫から出版されている。

Heroic Failure 『壮絶な失敗』（2018）。フィンタ
ン・オトゥールの著書。イギリスの離脱を分析
したもの。2023 年 11 月現在、未訳。

Chapter 2

Gary Janetti ゲイリー・ジャネッティ（1966 〜）。
アメリカのテレビ番組脚本家・制作者。アメリ
カのフォックス・テレビの『ファミリー・ガイ』
（*Family Guy*, 1999 〜）やイギリスの ITV の『ヴィ
シャス』（*Vicious*, 2013 〜 16）の脚本で知られ
る。

Prince George ジョージ王子（2013 〜）。ウィリ
アム王子とケイト妃の長男。

Prince William ウィリアム王子（1982 〜）。国王
チャールズ 3 世の長男で、イギリス皇太子（Prince
of Wales）。

Kate Middleton ケイト・ミドルトン、ケイト妃
（1982 〜）。イギリス皇太子妃。

Carolyn Harris キャロリン・ハリス。カナダの
歴史家、イギリス王室評論家。主著に *Magna
Carta and Its Gift to Canada: Democracy,
Law, and Human Rights*（2015）、*Raising
Royalty: 1000 Years of Royal Parenting*（2017）
など。

Prince Harry ハリー（ヘンリー）王子（1984 〜）。
国王チャールズ 3 世の次男で、ウィリアム王子
の弟。アルコール中毒や差別発言などスキャン
ダラスな言動が多い。元ハリウッド女優の妻メー
ガン・マークル（Meghan Markle, 1981 〜）に
対する人種差別があったとして 2020 年にイギ
リス王室からの離脱を表明。2022 年には Netflix
のドキュメンタリーに出演し、2023 年に暴露本
を発表。その主張には多くの矛盾が指摘されて

いる。

Rude Britannia 『ルード・ブリタニア』（「失礼な
ブリタニア」、2010）。BBC Four が制作して
いるドキュメンタリー・シリーズ『ブリタニア』
(*Britannia*, 2005 〜 13) のひとつ。タイトルはイ
ギリスの愛国歌 'Rule Britannia'（「ルール・ブリ
タニア」（続べよ、ブリタニア））のもじり。

Beyond the Fringe 『ビヨンド・ザ・フリン
ジ』。イギリスの劇作家アラン・ベネット (Alan
Bennet, 1934 〜) らによる風刺レビュー（歌や
踊りのついた娯楽演劇）で、1960 年のエディン
バラ・フェスティバルで初演。当時の有力政治
家を風刺したために物議を醸した。

That Was the Week That Was 『ザット・ワズ・
ザ・ウィーク・ザット・ワズ』（1962 〜 63）。
BBC の時事風刺番組。司会はデイヴィッド・フ
ロスト (David Frost, 1939 〜 2013)。

Private Eye 『プライベート・アイ』。1961 年創刊
のイギリスの時事風刺雑誌。

Spitting Image 『スピッティング・イメージ』
（1984 〜 96）。ITV 制作のイギリスの風刺人形
劇番組。

Boris Johnson ボリス・ジョンソン（1964 〜）。
イギリスの政治家。保守党議員で元首相。保守
系高級紙『タイムズ』(*The Times*) を筆禍で解雇
された後、『デイリー・テレグラフ』(*The Daily
Telegraph*) の欧州統合懐疑派の急先鋒として頭
角を現した。度重なる人種差別発言や植民地主
義の礼賛でかえって右派の支持を拡大し、ロン
ドン市長に選出。2012 年のロンドン・オリンピッ
クでの成功を機に国政に返り咲く。EU 離脱を
推進して 2019 年には首相にまで上りつめるが、
スキャンダルにまみれて 2022 年に辞任に追い
込まれる。

Jonathan Coe ジョナサン・コウ（1961 〜）。イ
ギリスの風刺作家。ラジオドラマにもなった
What a Carve Up!（1994）などで知られる有名
作家だが、2023 年 11 月現在、邦訳はない。

Political Disengagement in the UK 『イギリス
における政治不参加』。イギリス政府が 2022 年
に発表した報告書。

The Windsors 『ザ・ウィンザーズ』（2016 〜）。
Channel 4 制作のイギリスのシチュエーション・
コメディ番組。イギリス王室の風刺で有名。

Charles III チャールズ 3 世（1948 〜）。イギリス国
王。ダイアナ妃 (Diana Spencer, 1961 〜 97) と
の結婚生活の破綻と離婚（1996 年）などで国民的
人気は高くない。2005 年にはカミラ妃 (Camilla
Parker Bowles, 1947 〜) と再婚。2022 年に実

母エリザベス 2 世 (Elizabeth II, 1926 〜 2022)
の死去に伴い即位。長年有機農業と気候変動に
取り組んできたことでも知られる。

Rishi Sunak リシ・スナク（1980 〜）。イギリス
の政治家。保守党議員で首相。詳細は Chapter
13 本文参照。

Theresa May テリーザ・メイ（1956 〜）。イギリ
スの政治家。保守党議員で元首相。2016 年にデ
イヴィッド・キャメロンの後を継いで首相に就
任したものの、EU 離脱が行き詰まって 2019 年
に辞任。

David Cameron Chapter 1 参照。

Liz Truss リズ・トラス（1975 〜）。イギリスの政
治家。保守党議員で元首相。ボリス・ジョンソ
ンのスキャンダルの後、首相に就任。経済政策
に失敗して 49 日で辞任。2023 年現在、イギリ
スの首相在任期の最短記録となっている。

Chapter 3

The Wonder 『聖なる証』（2022）。アイルランド
＝イギリス＝アメリカ合作映画。原作はエマ・
ドナヒューの同名小説（2016）。詳細は本文参照
（邦訳はオークラ出版）。

Emma Donoghue エマ・ドナヒュー（1969 〜）。
アイルランドの小説家・劇作家。オーストリア
のフリッツル事件に触発された『部屋』(*Room*,
2010) で脚光を浴びる（邦訳は講談社）。本文で
取り上げられた『聖なる証』（2016）の他に、ア
イルランドにおける 1918 年の「スペインかぜ」
のパンデミックを題材にした『星のせいにして』
(*The Pull of the Stars*, 2020) でも知られる（邦
訳は河出書房新社）。2023 年現在、カナダ在住。

The Great Irish Famine 『アイルランド大飢饉』
（1996）。アメリカのドキュメンタリー映画。ア
イルランド大飢饉に対するイギリス政府の対応
の失敗、それに続くアメリカへの移民を跡づけ
たもの。

Ireland's Great Hunger and the Irish Diaspora
『アイルランドの大飢饉とディアスポラ』（2015）。
アメリカのクイニピアック大学映画・テレビ・
メディア学部制作のドキュメンタリー映画。大
飢饉の社会的・政治的要因や影響を、北米やオー
ストラリアへの移民とその子孫に焦点を当てて
分析している。

Black '47 『リベンジャー・スクワッド──宿命の
荒野』（2018）。アイルランド＝ルクセンブルク
＝ベルギー合作映画。ジャガイモ飢饉を舞台に、

脱走兵を主人公による復讐を描く。

Arracht 『アラハト』(2019)。アイルランド映画。ジャガイモ飢饉を舞台に、司祭の要請で赤の他人を受け入れることになった漁師を描く。タイトルの 'arracht' はアイルランド語で「怪物」の意味。

Chapter 4

Kenneth Branagh ケネス・ブラナー（1960 ～）。北アイルランド出身のイギリスの俳優・映画監督。ロイヤル・シェイクスピア・カンパニー（Royal Shakespeare Company）で舞台経験を積んだ後、自ら主演・監督した『ヘンリー五世』(*Henry V*, 1989)、『から騒ぎ』(*Much Ado About Nothing*, 1993)、『ハムレット』(*Hamlet*, 1996) などのシェイクスピア作品の映画化で名声を獲得。監督・脚本を務めた『ベルファスト』(*Belfast*, 2021) でアカデミー脚本賞を受賞している。

Belfast 『ベルファスト』(2021)。アイルランド＝イギリス合作映画。詳細は本文参照。

Donald Clarke ドナルド・クラーク。アイルランドのジャーナリスト。『アイリッシュ・タイムズ』の映画評論とコラムニストとして有名。

Caitríona Balfe カトリーナ・バルフ（1979 ～）。アイルランドのモデル・女優。ドルチェ＆ガッバーナなどのモデルとしてランウェイに立った後、『アウトランダー』（後述）で主演を務めたことで女優としての地位を確立。

Outlander 『アウトランダー』(2014 ～)。アメリカのテレビドラマ。第二次世界大戦中に従軍看護師だった主人公が 18 世紀のスコットランドにタイムスリップする歴史ファンタジー。シーズン後半では舞台がアメリカに移る。

Judi Dench ジュディ・デンチ（1934 ～）。イギリスの女優。もともと舞台女優であったが、『007 ゴールデンアイ』(*GoldenEye*, 1995) から『007 スカイフォール』(*Skyfall*, 2012) までジェームズ・ボンド（Chapter 5 参照）の上司役（コードネーム M）を演じたことでも知られる。『恋に落ちたシェイクスピア』(*Shakespeare in Love*, 1998) でアカデミー助演女優賞を受賞。

Bobby Sands ボビー・サンズ（1954 ～ 81）。アイルランド共和国 (IRA) 軍暫定派の活動家。悪名高いメイズ刑務所収監中にハンガー・ストライキをおこない、66 日間絶食したのちに死去。

Gerry Adams ジェリー・アダムズ（1948 ～）。アイルランドの政治家。シン・フェイン党の党首。

Chapter 5

Brave 『メリダとおそろしの森』(2012)。ピクサー制作のアメリカの 3D アニメーション映画。中世のスコットランドを舞台にした王女の冒険物語。日本での興行成績は振るわなかったが、世界的には大ヒットした。

Harry Potter 『ハリー・ポッターと賢者の石』(*Harry Potter and the Philosopher's Stone*, 1997) に始まり、『ハリー・ポッターと死の秘宝』(*Harry Potter and the Deathly Hallows*, 2007) に終わるイギリスの小説家 J・K・ローリング（Chapter 14 参照）の 7 本の連作小説、およびそれを原作とする 8 本の映画の主人公。両親からたぐいまれなる魔法能力を受け継いだ孤児で、「闇の帝王」ヴォルデモートを打ち倒す。

James Bond 『カジノ・ロワイヤル』(*Casino Royale*, 1953) に始まるイギリスの小説家イアン・フレミングのスパイ小説の主人公。コードネームは 007。1962 年に始まる映画は最も高い興行収入を誇るシリーズのひとつだが、原作と異なるばかりかオリジナルの作品も多い。

Brigadoon 『ブリガドーン』(1954)。アメリカのミュージカル映画。内容は本文参照。

Culloden 『カロデン』(1964)。BBC 制作のドキュメンタリードラマ。1745 年のジャコバイト (Jacobites) 蜂起、カロデンの戦いを描く。ジャコバイトとは、最後のカトリック王となったジェームズ 2 世 (James II, 1633 ～ 1701) およびその直系男子を復位させようとした反乱軍のこと。スコットランドに多く、フランスの支援を得ていた。カロデンの戦いの敗北により壊滅した。

Mary, Queen of Scots 『クイン・メリー──愛と悲しみの生涯』(1971)。イギリス＝アメリカ合作映画。スコットランドのメアリー女王（メアリー・スチュアート、Mary, Queen of Scots/Mary Stuart, 1542 ～ 87）の半生を描く。プロテスタントとカトリックの対立と権力闘争の中、エリザベス 1 世 (Elizabeth I, 1533 ～ 1603) に謀反を企てたとして死刑にされる。

Highlander 『ハイランダー ── 悪魔の戦士』(1986)。イギリス＝アメリカ合作映画。首をはねられない限り生き続ける戦士の物語。16 世紀のハイランドで生を受けた主人公が現代で最終決戦に挑む。

Rob Roy 『ロブ・ロイ──ロマンに生きた男』(1995)。スコットランド作家ウォルター・スコット (Walter Scott, 1771 ～ 1832) の小説 (1817)

を原作としたアメリカ映画。1715 年のジャコバ
イト蜂起を題材としている。

Outlaw King 『アウトロー・キング──スコット
ランドの英雄』(2018)。イギリス＝アメリカ合
作映画。14 世紀のスコットランド王ロバート・
ブルース (Robert the Bruce, 1274 ～ 1329) の
半生を描く。

Robert the Bruce 『ロバート・ブルース』(2019)。
イギリス映画。ロバート・ブルースの半生を描く。

Braveheart 『ブレイブハート』(1995)。アメリカ
映画。国民的英雄ウィリアム・ウォレス (William
Wallace, 1270 ～ 1305) の半生を描く。詳細は
本文参照。

Edie 『イーディ、83 歳はじめての山登り』(2017)。
イギリス映画。詳細は本文参照。

Wilbert M. Gesler ウィルバート・M・ゲスラー。
アメリカの地理学者。主著に *The Cultural
Geography of Health Care* (1991), *Healing
Places* (2003) など。

Chapter 6

the Beatles ビートルズ。イギリスのロックバンド。
ジョン・レノン、ポール・マッカートニー、ジョー
ジ・ハリスン、リンゴ・スター（すべて後述）とい
うリヴァプール出身の 4 人からなる。1962 年に
デビューし、「プリーズ・プリーズ・ミー」('Please
Please Me', 1963)、「抱きしめたい」('I Want to
Hold Your Hand', 1963)、「ア・ハード・デイズ・
ナイト」('A Hard Day's Night', 1964)、「ヘルプ！」
('Help', 1965)、「イエスタデイ」('Yesterday',
1965)、「ノルウェイの森」('Norwegian Wood
(This Bird Has Flown)', 1965)、「イエロー・サ
ブマリン」('Yellow Submarine', 1966)、「ヘイ・
ジュード」('Hey Jude', 1968)、「ゲット・バック」
('Get Back', 1969)、「レット・イット・ビー」('Let
It Be', 1970) などの数々の名曲を世に出し、12
枚のオリジナル・アルバムは現在でも高い評価を
得ている。数々の有名音楽誌で歴史上最も偉大な
ロックバンドに挙げられているだけでなく、その
人気は社会現象となり、その言動は音楽や若者文
化の枠組みを超えて世界に多大な影響を与えた。
1970 年に解散。

Sir Paul McCartney ポール・マッカートニー
(1942 ～)。ビートルズのメンバー。ベースとボー
カルを担当。後述のジョン・レノンと組んで「レ
ノン＝マッカートニー」名義でビートルズの多く
の楽曲を作るが、「イエスタデイ」「ヘイ・ジュー

ド」「ゲット・バック」「レット・イット・ビー」な
どは主に彼によるもの。ビートルズ解散後も精
力的な活動を続け、映画音楽も手がけ、スティー
ヴィー・ワンダー (Stevie Wonder, 1950 ～) や
マイケル・ジャクソン (Michael Jackson, 1958
～ 2009) らとも共演した。反人種差別、平和主義、
環境保護といった信条を公言しているが、これ
は娘のステラ (Stella McCartney, 1971 ～) にも
受け継がれている。

John Lennon ジョン・レノン (1940 ～ 80)。ビー
トルズのメンバー。ギターとボーカルを担当。レ
ノン＝マッカートニー名義でビートルズの多く
の楽曲を作るが、「プリーズ・プリーズ・ミー」「抱
きしめたい」「ア・ハード・デイズ・ナイト」「ヘル
プ！」「ノルウェイの森」などは主に彼によるもの。
後述のオノ・ヨーコとベトナム戦争への反戦運
動もおこなった。ビートルズ解散後も「イマジン」
('Imagine', 1971) や「ハッピー・クリスマス（戦
争は終わった）」('Happy Xmas (War Is Over)',
1971) を発表するなど精力的な活動を続けてい
たが、1980 年に移住先のニューヨークの自宅前
でファンを名乗る男に射殺された。

The Beatles: Get Back 『ザ・ビートルズ：Get
Back』(2021)。イギリス＝ニュージーランド＝
アメリカ合作のドキュメンタリー映画。ビート
ルズのいわゆる「ゲット・バック・セッション」の
映像と音声テープから構成されている。「ゲット・
バック・セッション」とは、ビートルズ解散のきっ
かけと言われている 1969 年のセッション。

George (Harrison) ジョージ・ハリスン (1943 ～
2001)。ビートルズのメンバー。ギターとボーカ
ルを担当。ビートルズ時代にはインド音楽の影
響を受けた楽曲で知られる。アコースティック
ギターを主体とする「ヒア・カムズ・ザ・サン」
('Here Comes the Sun', 1969) は、現在では最
も再生されているビートルズの楽曲のひとつで
ある。ビートルズ解散後も精力的に活動を続け、
ギタリストとしてもロックの殿堂入りを果たす
が、2001 年に病没。

Ringo (Starr) リンゴ・スター (1940 ～)。ビート
ルズのメンバー。ドラムとボーカルを担当。ビー
トルズ時代に楽曲も残しているが、広く知られて
いるのはレノン＝マッカートニーの「イエロー・
サブマリン」や「ウィズ・ア・リトル・ヘルプ・フ
ロム・マイ・フレンズ」('With a Little Help From
My Friends', 1967) のボーカルであろう。ビー
トルズ解散後は音楽活動だけではなく、俳優業で
も知られるようになり、日本でも CM にたびた
び出演している。

Yoko (Ono) オノ・ヨーコ (1933 〜)。日本の前衛芸術家・音楽家。アメリカのニューヨークを拠点に活動する。ジョン・レノンと結婚する。ファンの間では、オノ・ヨーコがビートルズのメンバーの不仲のひとつの原因になったとよく噂されてきた。

Yesterday 『イエスタデイ』(2019)。イギリス＝アメリカ合作映画。詳細は本文参照。

Danny Boyle ダニー・ボイル (1956 〜)。イギリスの映画監督。代表作に『トレインスポッティング』(*Trainspotting*, 1996)、『スラムドッグ＄ミリオネア』(*Slumdog Millionaire*, 2008) など。

Oasis オアシス。イギリスのロックバンド。「ワンダーウォール」('Wonderwall', 1995) や「ドント・ルック・バック・イン・アンガー」('Don't Look Back in Anger', 1996) などの世界的ヒット曲で 1990 年代を代表するロックバンドになるが、2009 年に解散。ビートルズと同じくイングランド北部 (ただしマンチェスター) の出身であることから、しばしば比較される。

Ed Sheeran エド・シーラン (1991 〜)。イギリスのシンガーソングライター。「A チーム」('The A Team', 2011) がグラミー賞最優秀楽曲賞にノミネートされたことで注目を浴び、「シンキング・アウト・ラウド」('Thinking Out Loud', 2014) や「シェイプ・オブ・ユー」('Shape of You', 2017) などの世界的ヒット曲を送り出す。2023 年時点でグラミー賞をすでに 4 度受賞している。

(Antonio) Salieri アントニオ・サリエリ (1750 〜 1825)。モーツァルトと同時代のイタリア人宮廷楽長。イギリスの劇作家ピーター・シェーファー (Peter Shaffer, 1926 〜 2016) の戯曲『アマデウス』(*Amadeus*, 1979) では、モーツァルトへの嫉妬に狂う音楽家として描かれている。この戯曲はチェコ出身の映画監督ミロス・フォアマン (Miloš Forman, 1932 〜 2018) によって映画化された (1984 年)。

(Wolfgang Amadeus) Mozart ヴォルフガング・アマデウス・モーツァルト (1756 〜 91)。オーストリアの作曲家。数々の名曲を残している。

Himesh Patel ヒメーシュ・パテル (1990 〜)。イギリスの俳優。本文で触れられている初主演作『イエスタデイ』で有名。

James Corden ジェームズ・コーデン (1978 〜)。イギリスの俳優・コメディアン。トーク番組の司会者として有名。

Ana de Armas アナ・デ・アルマス (1988 〜)。キューバの女優。出演作に『ブレードランナー 2049』(*Blade Runner 2049*, 2017) など。

the (Rolling) Stones ローリング・ストーンズ。イギリスのロックバンド。ブライアン・ジョーンズ (Brian Jones, 1942 〜 69)、ミック・ジャガー (Mick Jagger, 1943 〜)、キース・リチャーズ (Keith Richards, 1943 〜) らを中心に 1962 年に結成される。「サティスファクション」('(I Can't Get No) Satisfaction', 1965)、「黒くぬれ!」('Paint It, Black', 1966)、「悲しみのアンジー」('Angie', 1973)、「ミス・ユー」('Miss You', 1978)、「スタート・ミー・アップ」('Start Me Up', 1981) などの数々の名曲を世に出し、2023 年にアルバム『ハックニー・ダイアモンズ』(*Hackney Diamonds*) をリリースするなど、現在でも第一線で活躍している。

(Bob) Dylan ボブ・ディラン (1941 〜)。アメリカのシンガーソングライター。「風に吹かれて」('Blowin' in the Wind', 1963)、「時代は変わる」('The Times They Are a-Changin'', 1964)、「ライク・ア・ローリング・ストーン」('Like a Rolling Stone', 1965) などの名曲を世に出す。2016 年に歌手として初めてノーベル文学賞を受賞した。

(David) Bowie デイヴィッド・ボウイ (1947 〜 2016)。イギリスのロックミュージシャン。前衛的な歌詞やステージで知られ、コンセプト・アルバム『ジギー・スターダスト』(*The Rise and Fall of Ziggy Stardust and the Spiders from Mars*, 1972) はとりわけ有名。『戦場のメリークリスマス』(1983) をはじめ、映画にも多数出演。

Chapter 7

(BBC) *Newsline* BBC 北アイルランドのニュース番組 (1996 〜)。

Rebecca Anthony レベッカ・アンソニー。カーディフ大学社会科学部博士研究員 (2023 年 11 月現在)。専門は子どもの精神的健康。

Child and Adolescent Mental Health 『子どもと思春期のメンタルヘルス』。ワイリー＝ブラックウェル社 (Wiley-Blackwell) が出版する児童心理・小児科学の査読付き学術誌。

Kazuo Ishiguro カズオ・イシグロ (1954 〜)。日本生まれのイギリスの小説家。映画化もされた『日の名残り』(*The Remains of the Day*, 1989) や『わたしを離さないで』(*Never Let Me Go*, 2005) などで知られる (ともに邦訳はハヤカワ文庫)。2017 年にノーベル文学賞を受賞。

Klara and the Sun 『クララとお日さま』(2021)。カズオ・イシグロの小説。詳細は本文参照。邦

訳は早川書房。2023 年 5 月、ニュージーランド
の映画監督タイカ・ワイティティ（Taika Waititi,
1975 〜）監督による映画化が告知された。

Oscar Wilde　オスカー・ワイルド（1854 〜
1900）。アイルランド出身の劇作家・小説家・
評論家。代表作に『ドリアン・グレイの肖像』（*The
Picture of Dorian Gray*, 1890）や『真面目が肝心』
（*The Importance of Being Earnest*, 1895）など
（邦訳は多数存在）。

Chapter 8

Danny Boyle　Chapter 6 参照。

Mr Bean　ミスター・ビーン。イギリスの俳優・
コメディアンのローワン・アトキンソン（Rowan
Atkinson, 1955 〜）が同名のシチュエーション・
コメディ番組（1990 〜 95）で演じるキャラク
ター。

Mary Poppins　メアリー・ポピンズ。オーストラ
リア生まれのイギリス人作家 P・L・トラヴァー
ス（P. L. Travers, 1899 〜 1996）の『メアリー・
ポピンズ』シリーズ（1934 〜 88）に登場する、
魔法使いの乳母（ナニー）。シリーズの邦訳は岩
波少年文庫から出版されている。

Emergency Ward 10　『緊急病棟 10』（1957 〜
67）。ITV 制作の医療ドラマ。最初期の医療ソー
プ・オペラのひとつとされる。

Casualty　『カジュアルティ』（1986 〜）。BBC 制
作のイギリスのテレビドラマ。医療ドラマとし
ては世界で最長記録を持っている。架空の都市
ホルビーの救命救急病棟を中心に展開する。

Holby City　『ホルビー・シティ』（1999 〜 2022）。
『カジュアルティ』のスピンオフ番組。

Paul Unwin　ポール・アンウィン（1957 〜）。イ
ギリスの脚本家。舞台の脚本や演出も手がける
が、一般的には『カジュアルティ』の脚本で知ら
れる。

Jeremy Brock　ジェレミー・ブロック（1959 〜）。
イギリスの脚本家。『カジュアルティ』の他に、
『シャーロット・グレイ』（*Charlotte Gray*, 2001）
などの映画脚本でも知られる。

Margaret Thatcher　マーガレット・サッチャー
（1925 〜 2013）。イギリスの政治家。保守党議員、
元首相。1979 年に首相に就任すると、国営産業
の民営化、福祉の削減など、新自由主義的な経
済政策を推し進めた。強硬な政治姿勢から「鉄の
女」（Iron Lady）の異名でも知られる。

Under the Knife　『アンダー・ザ・ナイフ』（2019）。

イギリスのドキュメンタリー映画。NHS が政府
によってどう変えられてきたかを探る。

The Great NHS Heist　『NHS 大強盗』（2019）。
イギリスのドキュメンタリー映画。NHS が政府
によってどう変えられてきたかを探る。

The Dirty War on the NHS　『NHS に対する汚い
戦争』（2019）。イギリスのドキュメンタリー映
画。NHS が政府によってどう変えられてきたか
を探る。

Tony Blair　トニー・ブレア（1953 〜）。イギリス
の政治家。労働党議員、元首相。1990 年代から
2000 年代にかけて「ニュー・レイバー」を掲げ、
労働党の首相でありながら新自由主義的な経済
政策を推し進めた。

Rishi Sunak　Chapter 13 本文参照。

Chapter 9

Call the Midwife　『コール・ザ・ミッドワイフ
──ロンドン助産婦物語』（2012 〜）。BBC 制作
のイギリスのテレビドラマ。ジェニファー・ワー
ス（Jennifer Worth, 1935 〜 2011）の回顧録を
ドラマ化したものだが、シーズン 3 以降は完全
にオリジナルのストーリーになっている。

The Ministry of Nostalgia　『緊縮ノスタルジア』
（2016）。オーウェン・ハサリー（後述）の著作。
詳細は本文参照。邦訳は堀之内出版から出版さ
れている。

Owen Hatherley　オーウェン・ハサリー（1981
〜）。イギリスのジャーナリスト・作家。建築お
よび政治に関する著述が多い。

Ken Loach　ケン・ローチ（1936 〜）。イギリス
の映画監督。社会の底辺に暮らす人たちに寄り
添う社会派リアリストとして世界的に有名。カ
ンヌ映画祭では、『麦の穂をゆらす風』（*The Wind
That Shakes the Barley*, 2006）と『わたしは、
ダニエル・ブレイク』（後述）で 2 度パルムドール
（最高賞）を受賞している。

I, Daniel Blake　『わたしは、ダニエル・ブレイク』
（2016）。イギリス＝フランス＝ベルギー合作映
画。ケン・ローチ監督の代表作のひとつ。詳細
は本文参照。

Sorry We Missed You　『家族を想うとき』（2019）。
イギリス＝フランス＝ベルギー合作映画。ケン・
ローチ監督作品。詳細は本文参照。

Chapter 10

Rishi Sunak　Chapter 13 本文参照。

Climate Crisis and the 21st-Century British Novel　『21世紀イギリス小説における気候危機』（2017）。21世紀イギリス小説に自然観の変遷がいかに反映されているか跡づけた研究書。

Astrid Bracke　アストリッド・ブラッケ。オランダの英文学者。主著は前出の *Climate Crisis and the 21st-Century British Novel* (2017)。

Ian McEwan　イアン・マキューアン（1948〜）。イギリスの小説家。代表作に『時間の中の子供』（*The Child in Time*, 1987）、『アムステルダム』（*Amsterdam*, 1998）、『贖罪』（*Atonement*, 2001）など（邦訳は中央公論社および新潮文庫）。

Solar　『ソーラー』（2010）。イアン・マキューアンの小説。利己的な物理学者を主人公とするコミカルな作品。邦訳は新潮社から出版されている。

Nutshell　『憂鬱な 10 ヶ月』（2016）。イアン・マキューアンの小説。胎児の視点から外の世界を描く野心的な作品。邦訳は新潮社から出版されている。

The Rig　『リグ──霧に潜むモノ』（2023〜）。アマゾン・プライム制作のイギリスの配信ドラマ。スコットランドの絶海の北海油田プラントで起こるサスペンス。詳細は本文参照。

Chapter 11

George Floyd　ジョージ・フロイド（1973〜2020）。アフリカ系アメリカ人。偽造紙幣の使用容疑で拘束された際、白人警察官の暴力を受けた後に死亡。この対応をめぐって大規模な抗議デモが起こった。

Edward Colston　エドワード・コルストン（1636〜1721）。イギリスの政治家・貿易商。詳細は本文参照。

Katharine Viner　キャサリン・ヴァイナー（1971〜）。イギリスのジャーナリスト。高級紙『ガーディアン』の編集長を歴任。

Cassandra Gooptar　カッサンドラ・グープター。ハル大学ウィルバーフォース奴隷解放研究所博士研究員（2023 年 11 月現在）。

Nicholas Draper　ニコラス・ドレイパー。イギリスの歴史学者。主著に *The Price of Emancipation: Slave-Ownership, Compensation and British Society at the End of Slavery* (2010) など。

Cotton Capital: How Slavery Changed 'The Guardian', Britain and the World　『コットン・キャピタル──奴隷制はいかに「ガーディアン」、イギリス、世界を変えたか』。詳細は本文参照。

Chapter 12

Amelia Gentleman　アミリア・ジェントルマン（1972〜）。イギリスのジャーナリスト。いわゆるウィンドラッシュ事件の報道により、ポール・フット賞を受賞。

Sajid Javid　サジド・ジャヴィド（1969〜）。イギリスの政治家。ウィンドラッシュ事件による前任者の辞任を受けて、パキスタン系イギリス人としては初の内務大臣となる。

Krishnan Guru-Murthy　クリシュナン・グールー＝マーシー（1970〜）。イギリスのジャーナリスト。『Channel 4 ニュース』の司会者として有名。

The Windrush Betrayal: Exposing the Hostile Environment　『ウィンドラッシュの裏切り──敵対的環境を暴く』。アミリア・ジェントルマンの著作。

Chapter 13

Rishi Sunak　詳細は本文参照。

Akshata Murty　アクシャタ・ムルティ（1980〜）。インド人実業家。多国籍 IT 企業の創設者を父に持つ。リシ・スナクの妻。

King Charles III　Chapter 2 参照。

Liz Truss　Chapter 2 参照。

Penny Mordaunt　ペニー・モーダント（1973〜）。イギリスの政治家。保守党議員。メイ政権以降、閣僚ポストを歴任。

Freddie Mercury　フレディー・マーキュリー（1946〜91）。イギリスのミュージシャン。本名はファロク・ブルサラ（Farrokh Bulsara）。ザンジバル（現タンザニア）生まれのペルシャ系インド人で、家族は革命を逃れてイギリスに移住した。ロックバンド・クイーンを率い、「キラー・クイーン」（'Killer Queen', 1974）、「ボヘミアン・ラプソディ」（'Bohemian Rhapsody', 1975）、「伝説のチャンピオン（ウィー・アー・ザ・チャンピオンズ）」（'We Are the Champions', 1977）などの名曲を残す。1991 年にエイズにより死去。

Sadiq Khan　サディク・カーン（1970〜）。イギリスの政治家。労働党議員として運輸大臣などを歴任した後、2016 年からロンドン市長を務める。

Apsana Begum アプサナ・ベガム（1990 ～）。イギリスの政治家。労働党議員。ロンドンのイーストエンド出身で、選挙区は『コール・ザ・ミッドワイフ』（Chapter 9 参照）の舞台となっているポプラー。

Brick Lane 『ブリック・レーン』（2007）。イギリス映画。モニカ・アリ（Monica Ali, 1967 ～）の同名小説（2003）を原作とし、バングラデシュ系移民女性の精神的成長と決断をなぞる。この映画には賛否両論がある。なお、ブリック・レーンとはロンドンのイーストエンドの一角で、現在ではバングラデシュ系移民が多く住む。

Bodyguard 『ボディーガード――守るべきもの』（2018）。BBC 制作のイギリスのテレビドラマ。アフガニスタン帰還兵の巡査を主人公とした政治サスペンス。ドラマとしての評価は極めて高いが、この Chapter の Listening Comprehension で話されていたテーマについては議論の余地がある。

Chapter 14

J. K. Rowling J・K・ローリング（1965 ～）。イギリスの小説家。『ハリー・ポッター』（Chapter 5 参照）のシリーズで知られる。

Maya Forstater マヤ・フォーステイター（1973 ～）。イギリスのビジネス・国際開発研究者。本文に記載された案件で一般的には知られる。

Harry Potter Chapter 5 参照。

Daniel Radcliffe ダニエル・ラドクリフ（1989 ～）。イギリスの俳優。『ハリー・ポッター』シリーズで主人公ハリー・ポッターを演じて一躍有名になる。その後はウェストエンドとブロードウェイで舞台経験を積み、2007 年には『エクウス』（Equus, 1973）、2017 年には『ローゼンクランツとギルデンスターンは死んだ』（Rosencrantz and Guildenstern Are Dead, 1966）のような難解な戯曲に挑んだり、独立系のアメリカ映画『アンダーカバー』（Imperium, 2016）に主演したりしている。慈善活動に積極的で、政治的発言も多い。

Emma Watson エマ・ワトソン（1990 ～）。イギリスの俳優。『ハリー・ポッター』シリーズで、主人公ハリーの友人ハーマイオニー・グレンジャーを演じて一躍有名になる。アメリカ映画『ザ・サークル』（The Circle, 2017）や『ストーリー・オブ・マイライフ／わたしの若草物語』（Little Women, 2019）などに出演。ファッションモデルとして

も活動する傍ら、政治的発言も多い。

The Witch Trials of J. K. Rowling 『J・K・ローリングの魔女裁判』（2023）。ポッドキャスト番組。詳細は本文参照。

Fantastic Beasts 『ファンタスティック・ビースト』シリーズ（2016 ～）。『ハリー・ポッター』シリーズに登場する教科書の作者ニュート・スキャマンダーの冒険と校長先生ダンブルドアの過去に焦点を当てた作品群で、イギリス人監督デイヴィッド・イエーツ（David Yates, 1963 ～）が監督し、J・K・ローリングが脚本を担当する。ローリングは 5 本の作品を予定していたが、2024 年2 月現在、4 本目以降の制作予定はない。

Tom Hooper トム・フーパー（1972 ～）。イギリスの映画監督。代表作に『英国王のスピーチ』（The King's Speech, 2010）、『レ・ミゼラブル』（Les Misérables, 2012）、『リリーのすべて』（The Danish Girl, 2015）など。

The Danish Girl Chapter 15 本文参照。

My Transsexual Summer 『マイ・トランスセクシュアル・サマー』（2011）。Channel 4 制作のイギリスのテレビ番組。7 人のトランスジェンダーの人々が週末に別荘に集まり、生活する姿を描いたドキュメンタリー風のリアリティ番組。

Boy Meets Girl 『ボーイ・ミーツ・ガール』（2015 ～ 16）。BBC 制作のイギリスのテレビ番組。男性と年の離れたトランスジェンダー女性との関係を中心にしたシチュエーションコメディ。トランスジェンダー女性役をトランスジェンダー女性が演じていることでも話題になる。

Chapter 15

Sunday Bloody Sunday 『日曜日は別れの時』（1971）。イギリス映画。ゲイの医師、離婚した妻、医師が恋する若い彫刻家の三角関係を描く。監督はジョン・シュレジンジャー（John Schlesinger, 1926 ～ 2003）。

My Beautiful Laundrette 『マイ・ビューティフル・ランドレット』（1985）。イギリス映画。パキスタン系の若者がコインランドリー経営に乗り出す。白人至上主義グループに入ってしまった幼なじみの恋人との、人種・民族を越えた同性愛関係も中心的なテーマ。脚本はパキスタン系作家ハニフ・クレイシ（Hanif Kureishi, 1954 ～）。

Sally Potter サリー・ポッター（1949 ～）。イギリスの映画監督。代表作に『オルランド』（1992）、

『耳に残るは君の歌声』（*The Man Who Cried*, 2000）、『ジンジャーの朝──さよなら、わたしが愛した世界』（*Ginger & Rosa*, 2012）など。

Orlando 『オルランド』（1992）。イギリス映画。ヴァージニア・ウルフ（Virginia Woolf, 1882 ～ 1941）の同名小説（1928）を原作とし、時代を超え、性別を超えて生き続けるオルランド（オーランドー）を主人公とした幻想小説。

Tilda Swinton ティルダ・スウィントン（1960 ～）。イギリスの女優。イギリスの巨匠デレク・ジャーマン（Derek Jarman, 1942 ～ 94）監督作品への出演、とりわけ『エドワード II』（*Edward II*, 1991）でのヴェネツィア国際映画祭女優賞受賞で注目を浴びる。『オルランド』（1992）、『ナルニア国物語』シリーズ（*The Chronicles of Narnia*, 2005 ～ 10）、『ベンジャミン・バトン──数奇な人生』（*The Curious Case of Benjamin Button*, 2008）など多数の作品に出演。

Lilting 『リルティング』（2014）。イギリス映画。息子を亡くしたカンボジア系の母親が、その恋人であった男性とともに喪失の悲しみを乗り越えていく。

The Danish Girl 『リリーのすべて』（2015）。イギリス＝アメリカ＝ドイツ合作映画。詳細は本文参照。

Eddie Redmayne エディ・レッドメイン（1982 ～）。イギリスの俳優。舞台経験を積んだ後、映画に進出。『レ・ミゼラブル』（2012）、『リリーのすべて』（2015）、『ファンタスティック・ビースト』シリーズ（2016 ～）などに主演。

Lili Elbe リリー・エルベ（1882 ～ 1931）。デンマークの画家。世界で初めて性別適合手術を受けたことでも知られる。

Queer as Folk 『クィア・アズ・フォーク』（1999 ～ 2000）。Channel 4 制作のイギリスのテレビ番組。ゲイの生活を主題にしたドラマ。その後、同じタイトルとフォーマットで北米版（2000 ～ 05, 2022）が作られる。

Heartstopper 『HEARTSTOPPER ──ハートストッパー』（2022 ～）。Netflix 制作のイギリスのドラマシリーズ。原作はアリス・オズマン（後述）によるグラフィック・ノベル（2016）。詳細は本文参照。

Alice Oseman アリス・オズマン（1994 ～）。イギリスのヤングアダルトおよびグラフィック・ノベル作家。代表作は本文でも取り上げた『HEARTSTOPPER ──ハートストッパー』。

▶写真・スティール
p. 6: ©Ink Drop/Shutterstock.com ■ p.11: ©Alamy/ アフロ ■ p. 17:（上段左）©Zack Frank/Shutter stock.com（下段中央）©lembi/Shutterstock.com（下段右）©Alamy/ アフロ ■ p. 19: ©Everett Collection/ アフロ ■ p. 23: ©IWM. Used by permission of Imperial War Museums, London, UK. All rights reserved. ■ p. 25: ©Alamy/ アフロ ■ p. 35: © アフロ ■ p. 42: ©rawpixel.com / Freepik ■ p. 47: ©Alamy/ アフロ ■ p. 51: ©Yau Ming Low/Shutterstock.com ■ p. 53: ©Greta Gabaglio/Shutterstock.com ■ p. 55: ©Everett Collection/ アフロ ■ p. 58: ©abcbritain/Shutterstock.com ■ p. 59: ©Tom_Sanderson/Shutterstock.com ■ p. 65: ©Alamy/ アフロ ■ p. 71: ©Alamy/ アフロ ■ p. 77: ©Alamy/ アフロ ■ p. 83: ©TTL Deez/Shutterstock.com ■ p. 84: ©Greg Allen/Invision/AP/ アフロ ■ p. 90: Moviestore Collection/ アフロ ■ p. 91: Mary Evans Picture Library/ アフロ

▶挿画
p. 10: 板倉厳一郎

Reading Post-Brexit Britain
ブレグジット後のイギリスを読む

2024 年 4 月 10 日　初版第 1 刷発行

著　　者　Christopher J. Armstrong／Anthony Piccolo／板倉厳一郎

発 行 者　森　信久
発 行 所　株式会社　松 柏 社
　　　　　〒102−0072　東京都千代田区飯田橋1−6−1
　　　　　TEL　03 (3230) 4813（代表）
　　　　　FAX　03 (3230) 4857
　　　　　http://www.shohakusha.com
　　　　　e-mail: info@shohakusha.com

装　　幀　小島トシノブ（NONdesign）
印刷・製本　中央精版印刷株式会社

ISBN978-4-88198-789-6
略　　号 = 789